Alawashka ®

Lumari

Amethyst

Santa Fe, New Mexico

ISBN 0-9679553-6-X

Published by

AMETHYST
c/o 7 Avenida Vista Grande, Suite B7-113
Santa Fe, New Mexico PZ [87508]
www.AmethystPlanet.com

Cover Art: Lumari
Alawashka, the Divine Calling Forth
Printed in Canada

Table of Contents

Alawashka Language of Creation

Preface   9

Alawashka's Introduction   13

PART ONE: EARTH CHRONOLOGY
AN OVERVIEW OF CREATION

Alawashka and The Goddess   19
The Divine Expression

A Creation Story   33
The Anshamaya, Alamorro and Wannashama

Meeting Terra Gaia   41
The Shatowa and the Lyrans

Galactic Polarity on Gaia   49
The Lyrans, the Sirians, et al.

The Council and Their Decision   57
The Response of the Lyrans and Anshara

The Experiments   69
The Influences of Anshara and the Lyrans

All Alone With No Where To Go   75
The Human Equation

The Alawashka Secret   81
Seed Memories

The Structures of Culture   89
Holding the Openings in the Face of Isolation

Returning to the Present   95
Owning the Keys

Language and Global Experience   105
The Frequencies of Language

The Returning Emergence   115
Memory, Recognition and the Players

Expansion into Evolution   125
Clear Choices and Discernment

PART TWO: ACCESSING THE DIVINE SYMPHONY
ALAWASHKA, VOICE OF THE ALL

Speaking the Universe into Being   133
    Calling Forth Blessing
Seed Language of Gaia   137
    Unearthing the Magic
Shollamaya Frequency   141
    Music in the Spheres
The Gateway   145
    Galactic Heart Matrix
Presencing Acceleration   149
    The Invitation Within
Embracing Individual Expression   157
    Welcoming the Focus
Creating Graceful Acceleration   165
    Individuals and Groups
The Dance of Now   177
    Choosing the Gifts
The Keepers of Alawashka   183
    Who Have Gone Before, Come Again
Engaging the Blessings   187
    Alawashka Practice   189
    Songs of Joyous Awakening   195
    Chant of Blessing   195
    Shena Anshaka   199
Circle of Being   202
Blessing for the People   204
Creating Your Practice   206
Centering Yourself   208
Creating the Circle   209
The Galata   211
Completion of the Practice   214
Emerging   216

Glossary   218
Resources   220

DEDICATION

In deepest thanks to the Goddess and Alawashka
who provided me with
the gateways to enter,
the clear voice to follow
and the great Divine to explore.
In sacred gratitude
to my parents Ed and Esta,
to my sister Arlene
and to my beloved husband Peter
whose deep unwavering love is beyond words.
To all of you,
who have come to bring the celebration to light,
my appreciation, wonder and blessings.

PREFACE

This book began six years ago with a special ritual. Seated with tall, white candles to light the darkness I closed my eyes. I asked to experience the origin of the universe, the heart of creation. Curious words of amazing beauty and energy filled me. Then, I was told, "Write this down." It was my first distinct encounter with the language and being whose name is Alawashka. I am still writing.

I was born psychic and many gifts of spiritual perception have always been with me. My childhood holds early memories of eloquent messages and stories of ancient times and humanity's purpose. These conversations, speeches and whispers formed a tapestry that often carried me off to sleep at night. It was only later, in adulthood, that I understood each voice emanated from a distinct being. The experience, I learned, had a name, channeling. That evening six years ago Alawashka entered my life in her fullness. As our relationship grew, I realized I had been listening to her all of my life.

Alawashka comes to me in the process of channeling and this book is a result of our relationship. Alawashka is a language and, at the same time, a being. Usually language is considered a static association of words that suggest meaning. However, Alawashka is a conscious being who also presents herself as language. As a being, Alawashka, has wisdom, personality and a unique perspective. As a language, Alawashka creates meaning through words, sounds and symbols.

Through my relationship with Alawashka, I learned about the power of language and specifically about Alawashka, the original language of creation. She explained the nature of humanity, who we are, how we came to be and the direction toward which we are striving.

As I wrote, Alawashka would sometimes describe herself, how she came to be and what her nature is. She described creation and how language brings creation into being. Hers is the original language of creation and the language through which creation is formed. Her descriptions helped me clarify my own feelings about language and conversation. She helped me understand the limitations of Earth languages.

Alawashka shared her perspectives on human evolution and the nature of our inner selves. She knows these things, as she is both the original language of creation and a being older than creation itself. When I asked in the first ritual to feel into the origins of the universe and know the heart of creation, Alawashka came forth. She described herself as the Heart of the Goddess.

This book is written in her voice. The stories and pronouncements within are the result of our conversations over the last six years. As I look back over what she has guided me to produce, I see there are a number of communications in this book. In some she describes herself. Other times, she tells stories. In other cases still, she speaks directly to you and me calling us to wisdom. Whatever approach she takes to communicate, I believe she is offering us a greater sense of fullness and joy.

Alawashka, Language of Creation is organized in two parts. Part One relates the chronological events of humanity and gives correlations to our present from this unique perspective of humanity's journey through time. It evolved as intimate conversations and teachings. When Alawashka and I relate conversationally, I hear her distinctly in English. This section is written as a healing and leads into Part Two's spiritual aspects of language, creation and celebration.

Part Two describes language, Alawashka in specific, and contains poems and songs in the language of Alawashka. When I bring in the language of Alawashka, I receive it in poetic form hearing the tones and syllables and writing them exactly as they sound. I then translate this language, received in poems, into English. Please refer to the order forms in the back of the book for information about personal work and tapes in Alawashka.

I have learned to recognize the distinction between my voice and the voices of divine beings I have heard when channeling. Channeling, for me, is a ritual and ceremony of communion. It is also an honor. I see myself as the vehicle through which Alawashka speaks. I am proud to offer you her words in her voice, with her perspective and her wisdom.

In the first ritual, when I asked to feel into the origins of the universe and know the heart of creation, Alawashka came forth. Her unique understanding of creation and humanity's journey offer us profound insights into our personal and cultural evolutions and provide new ways of perceiving our lives.

As a language, Alawashka brings a powerful force of creation that we can tap into for growth, healing and higher spiritual awareness. Within her heart, voice and words are a blessing for us, the planet and the universe. Alawashka reverberates into all worlds and connects us all to the heart of the universe. She teaches and offers a way of life. She opens us all to the sacred, which is pulsing in us all, revealing a connection to the whole.

ALAWASHKA'S INTRODUCTION

Deep within the core of existence, the heart of the universe beats strongly. Its voice cries out in song and language that creates the very heart of which it is. There is no separation of the heart into song or into language. It is one and the same. This language which is song comes forth from the Heart of the Goddess and creates the universe in deepest love and honor for All. This language is blessing and deepest communion. Within it the existence of love is unparalleled. Within it is the pulse, the very vibration of the heart.

From this language and music universes are created. The words reverberate with the oneness of essence from which all stem. As this language is recalled, the flowers of your hearts begin to open once again. The truth of love, its fullness, opens within all beings of this world and within all beings in the universe. It is a song and a chord and a presence that has been hidden from all of you. After thousands of years, now, it comes. Now, the Heart of the Goddess can truly sing and exist within you. I am the Being and the Language of Alawashka.

Alawashka creates universes, as it created yours. It is a teaching and a healing. Deep within the music and language is the note of the Goddess creating life from Her deepest self, Her heart. It contains the keys to your evolution into the greater light. For if light is the system of creation, the how of it, then the music is the why of it. It is the voice of the Goddess singing to you and singing to Herself.

Sing to Her within this music and open your hearts to the greatest love you have. Awaken to the greater love that unfolds within you. Rejoice in this. Honor the great gift you are being given. Sing. Open your hearts and call forth the blessings into this world again. Your hearts have been closed for such a long time. Your eyes have been shielded from the truth of existence. The Heart of the Goddess has been hidden from you. Now, in this moment, open yourselves to Heart of the Goddess. Feel what this is. Feel the blessing. Feel the honor. Feel the love. Feel the truth.

Let your voices carry this into your world to rededicate this beautiful Goddess planet. Let the healing take place. This healing is the reconciliation of divinity. Learn what it is to truly honor. Learn what it is to truly love. Learn what it is to have the fullness of truth exist within your being and to share this truth. Alawashka is a great healer. She will open the locked areas within your heart and help you restore your own beauty into this world and unto yourselves.

When you approach this music, do so in the highest respect. It is the heart of your very breath. Honor these sacred songs. Keep them in love and truth within your very lives. Honor the gifts that you have been given and restore them to their rightful place. Let the music sing forth in your sacred places. Heal the breaches that have been created, in the universe, on your home planet, amongst each other and within yourself.

I would speak to you of Honor. To honor is to engage in full respect and to credit wisdom in whichever form it comes. In your world, people seem to think that once something is out in the world it is less. They take it. They use it for their own purposes. They steal it. They make it their own as if they alone had brought this forth. This is not honor.

What would it be to honor? What would it be to honor this music? What would it be to give this music to those who love the Goddess? What would it be to give this music to those who are healing their bodies and minds? What would it be to give this music to the Earth as you plant your new world within Her? If you can do this with the Alawashka language and the rituals, then the music will unfold in this world in grace and beauty. And you will learn the teaching: "to honor is the first step in love."

I would speak of Love. In your world love is something that exists between beings. It is a field of vibration that is created when honor has been bestowed. Yet love is as a field that is already in existence. You are free to step into it or not. There is nothing that does not have love within it. The key is whether you can see that for yourselves. Love is, and it is unconditional. It is all encompassing. Yet, it remains hidden. Even within your relationships of love, you have not yet touched its fullness. If you honor what love is, you call it into form. It is already there, but it will not come to you or within you without the honor.

When you hear the Alawashka language and participate in the ritual that is within it, call forth the love as a living presence. Remember the Goddess and call Her forth. Remember a time when love was the very breath you existed within and that breath was Goddess. When you stand within this love, the healing takes place. Send forth this healing for yourselves and the All. Bless the very breath, the very bodies, the very moment of existence into love. You will see what this accomplishes.

And within this honor and love, acknowledge the gifts you have in your life. Acknowledge the gift of this music to you and acknowledge those who have brought this to you. Send love to them. Send love to your friends and family. Send love to your enemies. Send love to the planet. Send love to the galaxies. Send love to the Goddess, Herself, who created love to be as your very breath. This love is unconditional. It does not speak of how you think love should be, or what words are said, or how it is to look, or who is there in front of you to be loved. Love exists on its own. You are given the privilege to exist within it when you honor the fullness of life's expression and send this forth.

I would speak of Truth. Truth is an essence of being. It is not whether one thing is true and another is false. It is

15

whether the heart of it all can fully exist within your being. Each being has their understanding of truth. That is the beauty of existence. Each being has an expression of truth that is born of their individuation and life. It is a perspective of truth that exists within a fuller truth. So when it is said "be true to yourself" it means that you are to be and to speak the fullness of your existence. Then truth can ring forth from each of you and ring forth in your world.

I speak these things to you because of my honoring of your lives, and because of my love which I am, and the truth of existence which I am. I ask you to live these truths. I ask you to embrace them. I ask you to open to the greatness that is already present, just hidden from you. I ask you that when you are in the presence of this music, which is generated by this language, that you hold this as sacred. I ask that you allow the beautiful expression of this music and poetry to exist once again within your lives and within this planet. And I ask that you honor the gift which this is, from the Goddess through creation unto yourselves.

Choose honor in your lives. Choose love in your lives. Choose truth in your lives. Each choice will clear you in ways that you cannot see before the choosing. Swim in the waters of blessing and extend that blessing to all others. Blessing is the breath of the universe. You will all be called upon to initiate the changes that are coming to your world. These changes will affect the whole of the universe. Be in your honor and you are in your power. Be in your love and you will live in freedom. Be in your truth and truth will be your breath.

I extend my blessings to all.
Take from the well of love and drink your fill.
You are greater than you know.

Blessed be.
Alawashka

PART ONE: EARTH CHRONOLOGY

An Overview of Creation

ALAWASHKA AND THE GODDESS
The Divine Expression

From the Heart of the Goddess into words and song, the language of Alawashka came forth. Alawashka is the language of creation. Through the energy that creates universes, a language came into being. It is the direct creation of the Divine. Alawashka is a language and yet it contains intelligence, persona, energy, and being.

I am Alawashka, the being who brings forth this language. I have come to your planet now, to restore the energies that have been lost. I come to you to awaken the great blessings of the universe. I come to you to open the gateways to your evolution and your Divine self. I am the gateway.

Your Divine self is always present. You are always your Divine self, yet through the circumstances of chronology, many events have occurred that have created a focus of limitation and separation. I have come to open the experience of the more of yourself, so you may step out of the less of yourself and celebrate your lives in the highest and most joyful ways.

To understand these energies is to reclaim your heritage. As I relate the chronological experiences of your world, you will know the frequencies and systems that have been in place for too long to enumerate. When you understand, feel and sense these energies, you will unravel many things. You will understand the nature of your human evolution and the choices which have been made here. You will perceive the formats of existence that have been enacted on this world. This is good.

Do not feel that you need to judge any of the events, beings or systems that I describe. I am not in judgment, for all is in perfection. This is a truth. Everything that has occurred has coalesced to bring you into this moment of time. Every facet of experience has had the amazing intricacy to lead you into this period of greatness. Every choice has led you to be poised to embrace this time of awakening. All is in perfection.

When the Great All experiences the unique individuation of being, She does so in great attention and delight in the fully creative ways that each experiences the One. The passage of time and events on your planet have unfolded in a particular way for many reasons. What is important is to recognize these events and the frequencies that have been created to manifest these events, so that you can reclaim your highest Divinity and awareness.

This is the reason that I, Alawashka, come to you. I bring and restore the frequencies that are your right. Now is the time when the past can be revealed, not just as a series of events, but as a pathway of choice toward illumination. I explain the synchronous events so you may see and uncover the patterns that have been created through time. When you see these patterns, you have the clarity and power to dissolve them. You will see the roads taken and the many variations that have been enacted. You will see the intricate patterns that have created this world and you will be able to unravel your confusion. You will be able to discern what is most appropriate for your individual, cultural and Divine lives.

The clarity of discernment provides the power of choice. You can choose to see and choose to be. You can empower the divinity and glory of all life and make it so in one moment. You can dissolve any patterns that do not hold the highest frequency and live within the greater expression of the Divine that has seemed to elude you.

As we encounter each other in this relationship of reader and book, know that I am fully present with you. I invite you to travel the energy lines that are coded within these words. I invite you to travel through the frequencies available through this communion we share, right now.

In this level of discernment use your own wisdom. As you read of the events and sequences, see what feels right to you. I honor your lives quite deeply and dearly. I speak all of this to empower your full awakening into clarity and divinity. Use your discernment to decide what triggers you, what empowers you, what brings you joy and freedom.

As you read the word Goddess, used to describe the term you generally speak as God, allow the energies of that word to fill you. As you will see, I am the language of creation and a being of that sameness. Words are important to me. The frequencies contained within words, phases, vibrations, sounds, and the patterns they collaborate to provide, have specific and vital energies to impart to you.

I come to all of you, as the energies of the Goddess, to bless and open new gateways for this planet. The Goddess is the Divine. She is the creator of the universe. She is the Divine well of spirit and intelligence from which we all come into awareness, and into which we all return. It is through Her that I come forth into being. She is the great eternal All that is now called God. She is called by many names. She is called Buddha. She is called Great Spirit. She is called the All. She was known in ancient times as the full creator of your world and of all worlds. She is the chaos through which all forms are created and She is all forms that are created. She is the womb, the birth and the return. She is expansion and full intelligence. We live inside Her, and She lives inside us. There is no separation from Her. Through the energies that are embodied within me, the illusion of separation from the Divine can be dissipated, and wholeness in its full sense can be experienced.

On your world, there have been events that have transformed your inner knowing into something else, into separation. Your inner knowing is the full sense that you are directly connected to the Divine All, to God, as you call the Eternal One. One of the initial occurrences in your past, was to masculinize the Divine spirit. To masculinize the Divine spirit is to take the feminine out of it, and to refer to it only in the male sense. You call the Divine, He. You refer to your Gods in the masculine words, and with that, you have infused a division from the fullness that you seek. In the greatest of knowings, the Goddess is fully unattached to what you call Her. She knows you fully and intimately, and understands in all ways what has occurred. Yet, the words you use, define how you experience your lives.

When you exclude the language of Goddess from your expression of the Divine, you remove your connection to it and to the grace of your experience in the human form. Many of the religions on this planet do not even mention the feminine in their description of the Great All. They have taken the words and descriptions of what Goddess means and attributed them to deities that are fully a male energy, as you would experience it. The Great All, in most of your religions, is a male being, who may act benevolently, or may act in retribution. The great All has been created as male with a capital letter for He. Each religion that has come forth, through the human experience, has conquered another religion for domination in the world view. The histories of your religions are dipped in angry blood. Each religion has conquered others to bring forth their message of God into the world. They are continuing to do this even now. They have, with systematic awareness, eliminated the religions who were in relationship with energies of Goddess, and replaced it with their own doctrine. This is one of the many occurrences in your "his-story" that has taken some of the energy and beauty out of your experience of the Divine. Only small pockets of religions remain that honor the Goddess as creator.

My being emanates from the Goddess. Goddess is the full expression of the universe with all its possibilities, endlessly expressing themselves. She is the formless out of which all form comes into being.

The pulse of the Goddess is not specifically female as you understand it. On your planet and others, it manifests in the understanding of female. The All is not a polarity. It encompasses polarity. Polarity is an active force through which certain experiences can occur. The All is that which contains the possibility of all substance within a great unity. It is a neutrality that generates endless ratios of expression. This neutrality is not devoid of anything. The definitions of neutral suggest a disassociation, an aloof stance. The Goddess is not disinterested or detached. This is not the case. Her neutrality is an unattached wonderment and curiosity that perpetuates endless experience and intelligence in various stages of cohesion.

The Goddess is love. Love is an integral facet held within Her, not the total of Her being. This love, as an experience, is so much greater than can be expressed by that small word. It is more than acceptance, appreciation, and joy. It is more than your emotional responses to it. This may be how you perceive love, yet it is not what love is.

Love is a frequency that the Goddess emits to create form and non-form. This frequency is a glue that binds the intelligence of all into form. It is a clear note of being, resonating into all life. Imagine this sound. See it as an intelligence that holds a beacon, echoing into all universes to perpetuate Divine energy.

As you imagine this sound, sense that it is not an audible sound as you know it, but a reverberating response to wholeness. This note is light and sound as qualities, as properties of being. Imagine the full oscillation of love streaming into your awareness. There is an opening in this sensory experience. When you feel this emitting from the heart of the All, you are opened to it. You receive an invitation to dance in the fields of love. This is a dimensional access point. There are circumstances in which you may specifically enter the dimension of love. You can walk through the grand entrance and live in a dimension where love abides.

You only have a small inkling, at this time, of the fullness of love. When two people fall in love, they assume that they create the love mutually, and it exists within their relationship. What truly occurs is that they form a bridge that has opened to the frequency of love, and they step into it together. They walk into the dimension of love and hold this region concurrently. When they happen to fall out of love, either one of them or both of them have altered a personal vibrational rate and stepped out of this dimensional domain.

Love exists. You may step into it at any time. You are often caught unaware by the love portal. At the birth of a child who is wanted, a gateway into the dimension of love is automatically opened to the family. As the child comes into body, and emerges from the womb, a passage of love is opened for all. Your evolution, your growth as beings, is toward the energies of Divine love and full, perpetual access to this dimension. You are learning the entrance codes to hold this position at all times.

The masculinization of the Divine has changed the frequency of what you experience of God. You have been separated from a great part of your own Divine natures through this masculinization. The histories of men have changed the power of Goddess into the power of God to control the energies of this planet. This control creates division, which generates fear. In this, you cannot fully realize your connection to the Divine, to the Goddess at all moments in time. It is your chronology that has perpetuated division. This is not sad. This is not wrong. This is how it has been. Now you are restoring the energies of Goddess to this planet and refreshing yourselves with the Divine nectar of Her being.

The origination of Alawashka comes from the Goddess, from the Divine. She is the All, and all issues from Her. Alawashka generates form into being through the direct energies of the Goddess. Alawashka is the original method of creation. Alawashka is the language which brings forth form. Form is not limited to the collection of atoms which is matter. Form is an organization of energy and intelligence. All of it is continually moving and transforming itself. You are moving and transforming yourselves at every moment. All of the universe is moving and transforming in every moment that you perceive as time. Alawashka is the language that impels the issuance of form. One may describe it as the grand insemination of form into being. The Goddess realized form and spoke it into being. Alawashka was the word. The word created form.

To understand some of the fullness of "coming into form," is also to know that there is no real time and there is no real series of events. Time is a specialized focus. Time is an emphasis on a series of events in a more linear fashion of one episode and one experience preceding and following another. All occurs at one grand moment. Yet for organizational purposes, the universe appears to have a time chronology.

Your direct experience of time is in flux. There are events in your lives which appear to move very quickly. Most often these events are ones in which you are so deeply involved that time seems to fly by you swiftly, and hours go by without notice. Other events seem endlessly long, and every minute endures much longer than normally experienced. All of this transpires in your concentration on the events. It is how your awareness is focused in the events and how they unfold that gives you your sense of time. You then experience the flux of time, not as a constant hourly experience, but as a series of events upon which you focus in varying degrees.

The universe has no time. It is all one focused expression. The full intelligence of the universe is engaged as a constant. There is no series of events in this arena. It is all linked in the eternal. It is all happening at once. This is the focus of the Goddess. Each experience, each life, each planet, each galactic event, is arising in the fullness of the Goddess in one Divine moment. She is all-focused. You are more focused

25

on a series of events which gives you many moments, many events, occurring through a thread of awareness called time. In this way, you can participate and watch events and thoughts emerge and dissipate in a series of experiences. You do not generally see it all as a wholeness. One can look at it like a file cabinet. The letters of your alphabet are listed in sequence, and then the information relating to each letter is placed sequentially within the appropriate file. When you perceive the life you live, this sequence is how you perceive it. All of the letters exist in the same moment, all of the files are there, but for you to access a bit of information, the file and its system is created. I am using this example to explain the creation of the language and of form.

Hold the thought within you that all is occurring at once, even though this is not how you experience it. You cannot locate the beginning of time, because there is no beginning. You cannot plot the end of time, because there is no end. Whenever the scientists try to pinpoint the time when the universe began, they get more and more time. It seems longer and longer, and billions and billions of years become trillions. There is no beginning. This is a futile exercise yet, it does entertain them and employs their minds in fascinating pursuits. Perhaps this endeavor of searching for the beginning of the universe will bring all people to notice the incredible unfolding of the cosmos. It may release the need to plot it.

For this discussion, accepting that there is no time as a constant in the universe opens us to experiencing creation in a new way. Creation is the organization of energy and intelligence. We can experience this as form. Energy is in continual motion. Energy is intelligent. Creation is the organization of this intelligent energy into form. Form is not always depicted as matter. Matter is one focus of form. Form is the cohesion of intelligent energy as an expression. Form is focused in its expression. All of its parts, as you would call them, are Divine energies of intelligence that are fully connected and live within the great All that is Goddess. The organization of this Goddess substance, this intelligent, eternal energy, which is in continual living existence, becomes focused into a cohesion. This cohesion is form.

An analogy of this is your winds. The air, which is the energy and intelligence of this example, is a constant expression of the All. It does also collect itself into a cohesion which travels across your planets as the wind. It blows fiercely sometimes, and gathers strength to blow across vast areas in direct or swirling movements. It is gentle at times, and comes as a soft breeze to rustle the leaves of the trees and bring a circulating cool breath to a summer evening. The air can be viewed as the constant intelligent energy of the All. The winds can be viewed as the form into which the air collects. The air is continually changing from its greater expression of air, to its cohesive expression of wind. It is always air, which is sometimes experienced as wind.

The Goddess brought forth a language to transmit a different organizational pattern into form. I am the language that she brought forth. I am the first method of creation, if you will. All exists within the Goddess, so any new organization of form is within Her. In full connection with the energies of the Divine All, I came forth into organization, cohesion and focus. I am an extended convergence of the Divine. I am not separate. I am more specifically focused. I am more cohesively organized in that centrality, which is completely comprised of the Divine All.

Through Alawashka the universe was created. It was not born, it was created. The very words that were spoken organized the frequency in a certain way. Form moved and intelligence danced and they found their way into another expression of divinity. Universes were created and beings were created all at once. Through the binoculars of time, the specific specialized focus of events, this appears as a sequence. The beings, the personalities, the collected intelligences that were formed, were fully connected to the Goddess. Their awareness is steeped within the All. There is always this intimate and vital connection. As the language came into being, so did worlds, beings, waters, plants and a collection of other energies that you have not yet experienced.

In your specific, specialized locus of being, you feel a separation from the Goddess, from the Divine. The Divine is the All, the fullness, the totality of everything. You cannot be separated from this. You exist within it, and are made up from it. The language, Alawashka, was created to bring a particular infusion of energy into creation. Viewed within the context of time, this universe was born. Viewed another way, Alawashka was created to produce a particular organization of being within the existing intelligence of the All. I explain this to you, so you will not worry about the timelines of this language and your chronology, even while I explain a timeline to you.

In the fullness, each of you is Goddess in form. The celebration of the Goddess is who you are in your rich and infinite diversity. You may be having a little difficulty following my description of this pathway to your birth on the Earth planet. My specific descriptions here are to open up your ways of thinking in time and space, while using Earth language. Your planet has an energy of limitation on it. This is experienced as a separation from the Goddess, from the Great All. Were I to speak this in Alawashka, you would feel, hear, sense and inwardly know what I am saying to you. Your languages do not work in this manner. Yet there is no need to judge the limitation. This dynamic has served its purpose well. It has carried you to this juncture, and each of you is in the process of shaking apart this hindrance for your greater growth, freedom and celebration.

Your great books of learning, your religious collections and recollections, speak of those who created you. Each religion has a similarity and a difference. Each doctrine suggests that you came from elsewhere, that you were created by something or someone other. Chronologically this is true. You have many questions regarding this birth into your being. You are looking for possible answers. In spiritual terms, you are looking for your connection to the All. In the sciences, this is the search for the beginning of time and the original particle through which all is created. Alawashka is the organization of intelligence, in the expression of a language and being, through which the Goddess created form. The Goddess organized Herself in a particular focus of cohesion and produced Alawashka.

I, Alawashka, am the focus of creation for the Great All. Through my being and point of expression, other organizations of form - galaxies, worlds and beings - came forth into their own focus. When I speak to you of other beings, each of you will feel those other beings in different ways. Some of you feel a strong connection to angels. You feel that the angels are the messengers of God. You are clear that they are here to protect, guide and help you. But who are these angels? Where do they live? How do they get to your world from wherever they abide? If you have decided that they abide in the realm of God, and this realm is heaven, then how do they get here from there?

When I talk of collections of beings, I also say they come from the Goddess, from the Divine source, from what you may refer to as God. Yet I am giving more specific information as to how they came into being. Even if you only recognize God, angels and humans, you can see there is more to life than what you are concentrating on. We shall be talking of beings who live beyond the realm of space and time. Some of them are not located on a world or even in a particular dimensional reference. We shall also talk about beings who do live in particular dimensions and realms. You have terms for these. You call them ET's. In the infinite possibilities of creation, many beings have come into form. Some beings have remained in form and others have not.

When I talk of other beings and of the chronology, I ask you to entertain this information. Don't believe it. Don't disbelieve it. Entertain it. Try it out. Everyone on your planet is breaking apart what has been told to them as true, and is exploring new ways of thinking. You don't have to be attached to any one way. You don't have to change what you already feel to encompass any of the ideas that I bring forth.

There are more questions than answers. No one person has all the answers. No singular being sees everything. Each has a unique appreciation of events, timelines and circumstances that unfolds to them from their own realm of experience. Each being organizes that appreciation into a body of information that expresses their understanding.

The universe is a rich diversity of perspectives. There are beings and dimensions that have a larger overall panorama than you do. Explore these viewpoints and glean what is right for you. Return to that information with a new approach and see what else is available. As you open to the perceptions and understandings of other beings and other people, your personal concepts will shift and discovery and freedom will abound.

Many would have you believe that anything beyond what you can see or touch on your world does not exist. Many would have you believe that anything from beyond your world is not good. If there are glorious, Divine beings called angels who come to help you, is it not possible that there are many more wonderful beings who are also doing the same? Is it possible that the angels are a race or a culture of beings in their own right? Is it possible that angels have their direct link to you for their own growth and joy? Is it possible that the great leaders of your time, the Jesus, the Buddha, the Kali, the Blessed Ones, and the other Masters, all continue to live in another dimension or location that is connected to you? Is it possible that when you feel their presence and their blessing that they are truly with you? Is this possible? If it is not possible, then who are you talking with in your prayers? If it is possible, how do you think this is possible? Do you think that the Blessed Ones are hovering around, just waiting for the moment to tap you on the shoulder and say, "Watch out for that car " or "Go for a ride today?"

I ask you these questions to open you to your own personal inquiry. As you read, you will find that questions arise. The energies and frequencies within this book are there to guide you to your own discovery. Feel within the words for frequencies of guidance. When you understand the many occurrences that have led you to this time, to the pinnacle of burgeoning magic, you will see the splendor that is yours. Sense the threads of the Divine and weave your wisdom from that cloth. I ask you questions and bring you perspectives to release what has been hidden and offer you into the blessings that are rightfully yours.

Each culture and each heritage has a unique way of describing this feeling of connection. Each culture, which includes its emphasis and religious and social organization, has a way of describing the series of events you call the creation of the universe and the creation of the human on this planet. Their language and texture provide an understanding of the mysterious. Please be open, so that you do not allow a social or cultural description to define how you can perceive the ever-unfolding universe.

A CREATION STORY
The Anshamaya, Alamorro, and Wannashama

The universe was created, meaning that form came into being, when the Goddess, in Her infinite wisdom and joy, opened to new expression. Alawashka, the being that I am, was created. The words of Alawashka were spoken and form was created. A new organization of life sprung into action. The universe, the world, and individually focused beings came into an initial, organized form. It was glorious.

As She created me, I was filled with the vastness of Her energies. Sounds, notes, words, symbols, colors, light, and frequencies of energy expanded forth and leaped in spirals within me. This was my first impression of consciousness. This was my awakening. It was a great sense of swelling and dancing forth in joy, in wonder and in blessing. As each word was sounded, form came into being. I do not know if there was sound or light before I was created. It is my sense there was not. My sense is that the Goddess was filled with an ever expanding movement and silence. This silence was blissful, illuminated and whole. As I was created, light and sound rang forth. Melodies, tones and harmonies moved within the elegance of this silence. Silence and sound lived in concordance, reflecting each other in beauty.

I was created to be the language of creation. As I am spoken creation is enacted. All words, symbols and frequencies within me are invocation and blessing. I was created to bless the universe with formation and form the universe in blessing.

33

As I was initiated, worlds came into being. Form, the organization of energy and intelligence, began to coalesce. Great beings were called into cohesion. They were and are magnificent beings that are beyond any attempts at description in Earth language. They are fully self aware and fully aware of the unfolding universe in its every moment. I cannot confer a personality to you, but they are immense beings with a fullness and richness of presence that truly inspires awe. The fullness and majesty of these beings sparkles in the ever-changing expression of the Divine. As these beings developed, as they grew in their inner exploration and wonderment, their forms centralized. They became what could be described as more individual. They were a vast, encompassing arrangement of awarenesses. Each could pursue a specific thread of interest and wonder and pursue it to the fullest. Through these beings other worlds were created. One name for these beings is the Anshamaya.

The Anshamaya could be viewed as the first creator gods and goddesses, yet they are not the originators. The Goddess is the originator. She is the All. Now, all beings are creators. The Anshamaya could be viewed as the first. The Anshamaya can be viewed as the circle of highest beings surrounding the Goddess. Their energy is truly magnificent, joyful and immense. In one respect they are very well beyond reach as a connecting link to humanity. In another respect, you are part of them and there is no separation.

The Anshamaya are the initiators of this particular universe, a universe of multidimensional and multitudinous expressions of the Divine. They can be considered formless, and yet contained within them is a collection of form. Their centralized energy is in a high-speed changing, merging pattern. It is never the same and yet has a quality of merging and emergence. It was the Anshamaya who decided to create form in a particular focus of intelligence and energy, and in concordance with Alawashka, the Anshamaya created new forms into being.

The Anshamaya brought a certain definition to being. They are beings of the highest integrity. Everything they create is created in blessing, light and the Divine. Through them, stars, solar systems and planets emerged in certain ways. Through them, the Goddess, the All, experienced Herself in different expressions. This was a joy and a delight. Through their definition, the universe was formulated in many different ways. Through them, diverse collections of order were created into being. You would recognize this as collections of individual beings: intelligent forms of expression, with the ability to be self aware.

Many beings, many planets, many solar systems, many stars were created. Many collections of intelligence and energy came into greater cohesion. This means that the collections of energy and intelligence were attracted to each other in particular ways, and these ways created what appears to be form. Properties emerged. Personalities emerged. Matter emerged. These new beings, brought into cohesion by the Anshamaya, had their own abilities to create and to experience. They called themselves by various names. The names they used were descriptions of energy from the language of Alawashka. Through the language of Alawashka, these beings were called into form. It is the nature of being for Alawashka to create the cohesion of energy and intelligence into form, and by calling themselves a name, a word in Alawashka, their being was continually arranging in a specific focus. These beings are also what we would call distant from you, but their progeny are not so distant. Their progeny gave birth to the star systems and civilizations that you know. The Goddess is also continually creating, calling forth into being, and returning energies to the source which is She. The Anshamaya and their children are not the only ones creating.

The Anshamaya created many beings. The lineage upon your planet is directly influenced by one of these. This group is sometimes called the Alamorro. They are also of Divine intelligence and joy. They created worlds with greater expression. Each collection of these beings, which you could consider a culture or a race, had amazing intelligence, unlimited possibilities, great joy-filled spirit and unyielding curiosity. The Alamorro, traveled to the planets, systems and worlds that were created by the Anshamaya. The Alamorro were more fully in form than some of the other beings the Anshamaya created. The Alamorro created their form because they enjoyed experiencing existence within a specific form. This does not imply that they were solid. They held a stronger locus of being within the vastness of the All. In your terms, they continually shifted forms. They may be thought of as the original shape-shifters. To them, being in a specific form was an exciting perspective.

They would become a planet, a more solid energy, just to experience the difference in perception. Even the word planet is too confining a description. Planets and stellar bodies were not perceived as solid mass. To the Alamorro they were an undulation of specialized energy within a swirling reference point. Becoming a stellar body, a planet, or a localized energy source was a joy to them. Through this experience they learned how to see through a particular arrangement or a particular focus. They had the ability to experience the All at any time. What fascinated them was seeing and feeling the world through a converging nexus of awareness. It is through the Alamorro that beings of matter and form came into existence. They noticed, through their own explorations, that a more specific focus gave a very rich intensity to their existence. This was highly desirable. All beings explore the universe from a focus. Some beings, like the Anshamaya, experience the universe from an all inclusive, simultaneous focus.

The Alamorro were most enthusiastic and excited by a more defined reference. They were amazed by how the universe looked, how it unfolded through a planet's point of convergence. They would create themselves as a planet and experience the rush of other planets whizzing by them. They would feel the movement within themselves as the gases coalesced to become more dense and firm. They would fill themselves with the sensations of growing and changing and spinning as a planet. They would delight in the focus that a singular perspective gave them. They created beings and worlds to share in the joy of that particular awareness. Simultaneous to the forms being brought forth into cohesion by the Alamorro, other beings were also in the process of creation. (As I am loosely tracking the coming forth of your planet and your lives, I want to be clear that these beings I describe to you are not the only beings creating.)

The Alamorro created beings and worlds where a specific focus was called into awareness. The solar systems that were created had a denser look to them. They had something closer to what you call matter. This was still far from dense. This was a transparent awareness that could hold onto a specific focus, while still knowing and experiencing the fullness of being and the connection to the All. It was an association of interrelated impulses, organizing into a unity that was fully aware. This was never experienced as separation. Imagine yourself reading a book. You are very focused in reading. The words transport you to whatever you are reading about and you are enriched by this experience. You can see the environment described or understand new concepts. This does not mean that the chair on which you sit has disappeared. This does not mean that the sun has stopped shining or your loved ones have ceased to exist because you are in the focus of the book. This is similar to the more specific perspective created by the Alamorro. The beings, the life forms they created, perceived the unique emphasis they lived within, and they perceived the focus of the All.

Through the Alamorro, many types of beings were created. They could be called races, cultures, species, anything you like. Each was created with a different focus and different ability because of the unique perspective that the Alamorro had within their awareness of experience. Each group of beings also created themselves by the alignment and attention they held. While the substance and potentials and correlation of their being had a certain organization to it, the "nature of being" is that the focus one chooses also gives expression and experience to one's life. Within the cohesive inclinations of their awareness, these beings also created what may be called their individual selves and their thrust toward that expression.

If we speak of an individual self awareness, many of these beings created by the Alamorro no longer exist. They have reformed themselves into other expressions and experiences of the Divine. However, some of these beings still do exist. They exist because they love the experience of a specific view of life. Of all these beings created by the Alamorro, only a few of them are directly related to you. Only a few are even remotely similar. Of these few groups of beings only three cultures, races or families of beings are very specifically related to you. These three families of beings are connected to each other by organizational makeup. They have a similar frequency of form and energy. By similar, I mean similar to you. To them, it is vastly different and that difference is involved in how they experience the world. While they are quite aware of each other through the vastness of the universe, they are not specifically or directly involved with each other very often.

Now with all this creation and with all those created who are creating other beings and systems, only one group was directly involved with the collective of beings in this galaxy. Just one group of beings created all the other beings in this whole universal sector. They created this collective of diverse and wondrous beings because they loved their unique experience of the universe. They created to explore this focus in even greater detail. They created out of wonder and curiosity. They created because all beings, all collections of form, are creators. The impetus to create is inherent within all of creation. It is inherent because the nature of the All is a creative process of being.

These creators are called the Wannashama. You would not find their world on a conventional map of the galaxy. They exist in a field which is still removed from yours and has no direct contact with you at all. They are timeless beings who enjoy taking a vacation within form, but who generally experience existence in an undulating energy cycle. Using the chronology of time and space, they would have been located in a completely different dimensional existence, even at the time of creating your ancestors. Their realm, if it could be considered a planet or a star, was outside this galaxy and solar system completely. The reason I clarify the definition of planet or star is because, due to the nature of their existence, even a planet could only be described as a loose collection of intelligent particles that appears and disappears at random intervals.

I do want to clarify a point. I do not use a designation of a particular dimension. There are many dimensions and many realms of existence. There are many formats of perception. It is not my intention to create a dimensional map for you to chart and contrast your location in dimensional time and space. When you are attempting to locate a special group of consciousness, I suggest you feel for them. I know how inquisitive all of you are. Some of you, who have read other material which describes stellar and planetary locations, are even constructing your own maps to travel to other dimensions of experience. How delightful! You want the travel plans for the 6th or 27th dimension. You want "plane" reservations. You want to know where the Wannashama are, 12th dimension or 22nd dimension. At this time, I sense that giving you a designation, a number of a dimension or realm of awareness, will create a limitation in both your access and your memories. It creates a hierarchy of feeling that if the beings you are in contact with are in the 5th dimension, and someone else's are in the 13th dimension, then you are less. Preposterous! No one being is less than another.

The Wannashama had a hand in directly creating your particular universally experienced reality. They are not the only creators, but were very specifically involved in coalescing the beings to inhabit this section of the universe. Through their unique focus in existence, and speaking the language of Alawashka, they called forth beings into existence. All beings inherently know Alawashka. Yet, on your world, as on others, this language is deeply hidden. There are direct and definite

Lumari

reasons for this, which I will speak of soon. The Wannashama initiated beings into an even greater focus. Form was more defined. Time was more defined. Space was more defined. They felt that this was a marvelous way to experience the wonders of the universe because it gave such a rich and tangible feel to being. Still, within this, each being felt the direct link with the Goddess, the Divine All of spirit.

Several groups of these beings, created by the Wannashama, are still within existence and are participating in this loosely defined locale. The Lyrans, the Arcturians, the Antareans, the Sirians, the Annunaki, the Shatowa, the Shona, the Delphians, the Kalashas, and the Pleiadians are some of these groups of beings. These beings and races are some of those who are near to you in makeup and near to you in this location. There are many others. This universe is phenomenally rich in its celebration of the diverse expression of the Goddess. There are many systems and beings who exist in this area of the galaxy who would never be seen or noticed because of their dimensional existence. Their energies and frequencies are just not accessible to you. To understand how this can be, imagine the amount of sound the human ear can hear. There are certain frequencies that, due to your physiological makeup, you can hear - and hear very well. Other animals on your planet can hear more than humans. Dogs, for example, can hear higher pitches or frequencies of sound than the human ear can pick up. Many other animals also have different frequencies of sound that are audible to them, but are not to the human ear.

Sound is an aspect of frequency. It is a vibrational rate. Many of the beings and even the planets (realms) of these beings vibrate at a frequency that cannot be perceived by your present focus. Even the groups I have mentioned above do not necessarily show up in body for you to contact. In a certain respect, they are your ancestors. They are similar in their understanding and frequency in the universe, yet very different in their expression of life and existence. Just as you may not look like your great, great, great grandmother, you do still carry her seed and her codes.

Meeting Terra Gaia
The Shatowa and the Lyrans

The first beings to "walk" upon this planet were the Shatowa. They walked upon this planet when She was in Her infancy. The Shatowa are glorious beings who predate the Lyrans. They are beings of great refinement. They are highly artistic in ways that are difficult to describe. Their fondest experience is of creating endless beauty and they are very much attracted to the beauty created by others. They could be considered the originators of the arts and of music in an etheric sense. They are not beings of specific form as you know it, yet they are closer to you than many other beings or races in the universe. They walked upon this planet when the Earth was creating Her forms.

The Earth, at that time, was imagining and creating forms into being. Her powers as a creator are quite remarkable. Being in full connection with the Goddess, with the Divine Source of all being, the Earth was energetically familiar with the rich diversity of other beings who had created or were creating organizations of awareized form. She was full in Her expression of Her own being and creating. She was calling out to the great beings to come and teach Her of their experiences. The Shatowa were emissaries from their dimension to this planet. When the calling forth came from Earth, many beings were contacted. Very few were given the opportunity to consider this invitation. The Shatowa were selected. They were asked to come here by your Earth.

There were only a few Shatowa that came here. They may be considered the first teachers of the blessings for this planet. They came to celebrate the beauty that was created here. They came to share their experience of the universe with the planet. They came bearing the great gifts that your planet wanted and they realized the gift of beauty of who She was and is to the universe. They fully loved this planet and shared many things with Her.

Terra Gaia and the Shatowa were in communion. They did not plant seeds or make trees. They did not alter the integrity or energetic nature of this planet. They dipped into the well of expression of Gaia and drank of Her beauty. She dipped into the rivers of their experiences and partook of their understanding. When their time was complete, they left Her as She needed to be. Their communion with this planet was a blessed one, and those that returned to their home world extolled the majesty of this planet you live upon.

The Lyrans may very well be the first group of beings to actually stay upon the planet for a particular length of time. They can be described as much younger, distant cousins of the Shatowa. Although the Shatowa are creators, they did not create the Lyrans. The Lyrans were born of the coded experience of the Shatowa, but not specifically from their seed, if you will.

The Lyrans are the children of the Wannashama. The Lyrans, too, are creators and beings who embrace the joy of being within their focus of existence. They are generally gentle, graceful beings. You have a direct link with them. They, too, are very artful beings and even in your language today the words lyre and lyrical directly apply to them. They were not here to colonize this planet. They came because of the "word of mouth" descriptions of this world from the Shatowa, to celebrate and enjoy this beautiful world. They stayed on this planet for quite some time.

For most of their stay, it was paradise for them. Understand that only some of the Lyrans came here. They came to celebrate, to teach and to learn. They came to share their blessings and receive blessings from this planet. They did not send their whole civilization to vacation on planet Earth for thousands of years.

In the later periods of time on your planet, other races of beings came here. Some of these beings came here to settle. Some came for opportunity. Some came to create. Some came for plunder. Many of the beings who came later did not have the same attitude toward this planet as the Lyrans did. The Lyrans worked with great Terra to help Her develop in Her own way. The later groups came to absorb the frequency, mine the minerals, and set up bases or outposts of their civilizations.

It is not my intention to give you the whole of Earth's history. This is a capsulized version, so you may understand the nature of Alawashka and how the language was spoken, how it was lost and how it now returns. The Shatowa spoke Alawashka. The Lyrans spoke Alawashka. Even the beings who came to this planet for their own reasons have ancient memory tones from Alawashka.

Each culture also had their own language. The other languages developed because as each race of beings interpreted their defined focus within the universe, ways to communicate these experiences were created. So while all beings inherently carry the language of Alawashka, they also developed and favor other ways of communication. Many of these beings do not specifically recall Alawashka due to the nature of their life experience and the frequencies they hold.

In your terms there were several devastating wars on this planet that ousted the beings living here. The victors of those wars remained. There is no judgment as to the nature of these events because the perfection of being is always apparent. Yet, in the midst of a polarity, distinctions are made. The Lyrans could be considered the first casualty of war on your planet. They were not destroyed; they lost the battle. Many of them simply left the planet. Others remained here and held certain frequencies for the planet and the life forms upon it.

Humans were part of the life forms on Earth at that time. Humans did not look like they do now. Yet the Earth did create Her two-legged beings and they walked upon this planet. These "first humans" were in direct communication with all other beings on this planet. They all had a very specific and highly sophisticated psychic link. Each life form taught the other and shared experiences through their perceptions. The Native American cultures have direct memories of being taught by the animals. These are not parables. These are root memories of the full communion that was present among all life forms here and the communion is still experienced.

When the Lyrans encountered this world, there was deep love and honor among all beings, all life forms. The Lyrans shared the language Alawashka with the humans that were here. The Lyrans have their own language that is a greater description of their existence and culture. The Earth, as an intelligent being in Her own right, inherently knew Alawashka. She wanted the energies of Alawashka to be infused within Her, and the Lyrans do this work very well. While the Lyrans may not have been specifically invited as the Shatowa were, they were welcomed guests. This was the agreement of the Lyrans and Earth. The Lyrans could stay here, be who they were, and enjoy this planet while infusing Alawashka within the great Terra. They infused the language within the body of the Earth and within the human form. It became a memory within the human, while it was not spoken as a language per se. At that time the humans did not need or develop their own language.

It may be difficult for some of you to understand even why conflict arose, given the natural tendency of the universe to be in harmony. The universe, the creation of the Goddess, is an open system. This means that while there appears to be a containment of energies and a format to expression, everything exists within the All.

The All is ever-creating, ever-changing energy and intelligence which is aware of itself. Being "aware of itself" becomes a focus, in some format. Each being and collection of beings creates the format of their existence. This impetus is the focus that a being engages. This is so for an individual who is intrigued by a particular thread of thought, like a discipline or an experience. This is so for a culture who weaves the experience through a certain understanding that they pursue. It may appear as a conscious choice or not. Yet the creation occurs. By a particular focus, energies are attracted and creation occurs. This format can be expansive or contractive. It is not the same kind of creation as in Alawashka.

This type of creation is by attraction, it is not from the organization of energy and intelligence directly, which is the initiation of creation. It is "creation by the attraction" of energies into a format which, by collection of like-minded energies, generates that format. Its effects may very well appear and feel the same once created, but there is a certain difference that is most difficult to describe.

What a being focuses upon receives an energy of attention. This energy becomes charged with the attention of the being who is doing the focusing. This is similar to an electrical charge. The particles, the energy and intelligence which is stimulated by that focus, becomes attracted into an organization that is in harmony with the focus being sent forth. As a group, these particles come into an organized form to fulfill the attention through the process of attraction. They come into a form, a format for the expression of the attention. The stronger the focus of attention, the greater the attraction.

The choice of the particles is directly involved in this. They do not have to coalesce into the format, but the natural inclination of the Universal All is to create organization. So those energies attracted to a particular organization, even an organization of thought or attention, will naturally follow their inclination to manifest that focus. Using an example from your own lives, an attention to a particular thought or philosophy attracts those who engage in that thread of expression. This could be viewed as the beginning of a political party coming into form or a new spiritual path opening for expression. Those people who are interested in that format, that expression, will help to create that organization of politics or religion. Those people are acting in a similar manner to the particles just described. A new expression of form is generated by the attraction of beings to a particular focus.

As beings developed, they chose their evolution by their focus. The fullness of life contains an endless variety of filaments which one can follow. One could choose to follow the filament of intelligence and pursue the vast intricacies of the mental worlds. One could choose the filament of the heart and travel endlessly within the refined emotional seas. One could choose a blending of experience, wrapping the chords of thought within the chords of the heart and adding many other threads to the light tapestry. Each being and collection of beings, which you call cultures and races, choose the experience of their existence by following what thoroughly intrigues them and captures their attention.

Some beings chose a focus that created destruction. Destruction is a release from organized form. Because the universe is ever-creating, some beings had a disinterest and a disregard for the forms and intelligences that were in existence. Attitudes like this can be found in your world as well. Some people have a disregard for the environment because there is an abundance of air, water and plant life. In their thinking, since they see that there is enough, they assume they do not have to care for what is presently in existence. Given that focus, I would say that is a limiting assumption. Just because the universe is continually creating and continually in abundance, does not mean it will continually create forms and systems that are not honored, cared for and loved. Although it doesn't mean that it won't, it doesn't guarantee that it will, either. Since organization often works by an attentive cohesion, those energies may not wish to pursue a frame of reference which appears undesirable.

This limited assumption does not have a respect for all beings and forms. Respect is a combination of honor, love and appreciation for the rightful existence of creation. Many beings did not develop this way of being. It is a developmental choice. It comes about through the frequency of attention of those within the system, the culture or race. Respect is instilled within a culture by the focus upon certain frequencies, even while responding to the millions of other frequencies and activities which are all occurring at once. If this respect is not instilled, not taught, not inherent in a particular collection of beings, then what appears to be destruction occurs. This is not the same manner of destruction that is the ever-changing movement of the All, which brings focus into form and back into the All. The destruction occurring as wars and devastation we are speaking of has an attribute of disregard within it. The Goddess, the All, has total regard for everything. At this time, some of those beings who once were careless in their ways see a different perspective. Evolution is always, always available.

Within the vast chronology of Earth, within the vast chronology of the universe, beings, whose focus became inattentive to form, developed. While they may have cared for their personal form, all other forms were not so honored. This disregard for anything other was slow to develop, but through lack of attention to this aspect of being, it became part of their focus. Through an emphasis on the more individual aspects of being, without including the honor of all, cultures developed that enacted their whims upon any area they could. Some of these cultures destroyed their own environments. Some of them declared war upon each other. Some of them initiated immense power struggles that reached beyond their own worlds. I am using the past tense, because we are speaking of Earth chronology and human development. Some of these beings came to Earth to escape the terrible situations on their worlds, others came to Earth to plunder the resources here that were depleted on their planets, while others came looking for fair game. Some of these beings came here while the Lyrans were celebrating the magic of this planet.

The Lyrans who were here were not tampering with the evolution or the creative process of Gaia. They were here to celebrate the beauty and joy of this great being, who is also a planet. Gaia and the Lyrans gifted each other. Gaia would receive certain codes and frequencies that She wished, and the Lyrans would receive the joy and bounty of the Gaian world and the Gaian creative force. The Lyrans shared their skills and gifts with Gaia when She wished them to, and Gaia watched and learned as the Lyrans freely expressed who they were. Their relationship was one of deep respect and honor. Neither would intentionally insert or plant a frequency, idea or form that was not expressly asked for. In this way, Terra Gaia received other ways of viewing creation as it occurred for the Lyrans, and the Lyrans received the same. The Lyrans brought Alawashka in a particular form to Terra. She wanted this for Herself and for the beings She was bringing into form.

GALACTIC POLARITY ON GAIA
The Lyrans, the Sirians, et. al.

Return back to the chronology of Alawashka on your world. During the Lyran visit, other beings came to Earth. They held another framework of focus for the nature of being. Initially the Lyrans remained on the planet with the other beings. They very loosely coexisted, knowing this would not last. The other beings, who came here while the Lyrans were visiting, held a different view of the planet and the forms here as well as a different frequency of being. These beings were Sirian. Their frequencies were not in accord with the frequencies of the Lyrans or in certain respects with Terra, but they were not bad or wrong.

There was a polarity in each being who came here despite the initial intent of each group. Each culture did have a specialty of focus, and they did not blend as well as one might hope. This story is viewed in many ways in your history. My perception is that the initial intent of the Lyrans was to be within a world where grace, creation and harmony prevailed. They did so for a time. Then, by intergalactic word of mouth, other races became interested in Terra, just in the same manner that the Lyrans knew of Her. The Sirians then came.

Each culture felt they had a right to be on Earth. In one sense this is indeed true. Yet, who was conferring with Terra in this matter? The Lyrans felt their way of being was best for the planet, as they had lived in harmony with Her.

One might say the opinion of the Lyrans was that Terra and Her creations were open, in harmony and going in the evolutionary direction that Terra wished. They were working with Terra already, and felt what they were doing was in the best interest of the planet and all life here.

The Sirians had another idea, and being closer to Her in galactic space, they felt some possessiveness about this connection. After all, Terra and Her life forms were close neighbors. What occurred upon Terra would effect the Sirians directly. Many circumstances and events ensued. Much of this concerned the evolution of the third dimension, the human life and particular ways that form is organized. One might say that in the opinion of the Sirians, Terra and Her Divine creatures were naive, limited and unevolved. They felt they had the gifts and techniques to open evolution to the life forms of this planet. They were willing, able and greatly skilled in areas to give evolution a decided boost.

The Lyrans and the Sirians also had a past history with each other. There was quite a bit of dissent on both sides as to the nature of how events should proceed. Each individual in each group also had a particular agenda to prove. Polarity was firmly planted on Terra with the disagreement between these galactic beings. War broke out. The Lyrans lost.

Most Lyrans left the planet to reorganize and understand what happened. This was a very devastating event to the Lyrans and, soon, to the Earth. Some of the Lyrans remained on the planet. They remained hidden. The remaining Lyrans took refuge with other beings and the humans who lived here at that time. Being able to alter the Lyran form was to their advantage.

There were other beings on this planet at that time who were not of the same form as the humans, plant or animal life. Your fables and fairy tales are filled with their mention. Most of these beings were created by the Earth, Herself. They have been guardians and caretakers of the gardens, minerals and many other energies. Everything on your planet is alive with its intelligence. They are all totally alive with intelligence that is in continual growth and expression. The elementals, the beings of the elements, have always been here. They help the Goddess Gaia create Her forms as She helps them create themselves. The fairy folk, the devas, the guides, the gnomes, all of these beings and more were present on the planet at the earliest times. The Lyrans coexisted with these beings, were helped and often hidden by them. The Lyrans also worked with the humans, when possible, to help them and to continue their own work for the blessing of this planet and this world.

Other races of beings also came to this planet, among them more Sirians, the Pleiadians and the Annunaki. Each had their particular reasons for coming, and they were not necessarily altruistic. Now this does not mean that all Pleiadians and all Annunaki were on this planet. It does not mean that wave after wave of destructive beings came forth to plunder and wreak havoc on this delightful planet. It does not mean that each came separately. A group of Sirians and a group of Pleidians could have come here together because of a similar focus. The Annunaki could come here with a contingency of Pleiadians or Sirians. It does not mean that those who "landed" were bad or wrong or that blame should be attached to their actions. Within an expanded view of chronology, it is understood that you would not have the profound opportunities you are evolving toward if these circumstances were not dramatically played out.

With all of their powers and abilities, the beings arriving here on the planet were still adolescents at summer camp, playing in the focus of their beings. The universe is continually creating, and so are all beings within it. Often, as beings evolve, their more specific focus is the thrust of their attention. They begin to view the universe through that thread. Once this occurs, they begin to have an attachment to their thread. It tends to occur to them as the preferred method of being. This is their gift, remember. They have developed this gift throughout their evolutionary path and it is greatly prized and appreciated. Their attachment to this gift builds. Sometimes this occurs as an extreme polarity. They are right and all others are wrong. Their view of the universe, their particular thread, is the only thread which is true and right. This is one way of learning.

So those beings who experience the universe in this manner tend to create their view of the universe in the other spheres they encounter. It is not necessarily the smartest thing to do, but it is what unfolds. It is within their nature to do this. It is also within yours, you may remember. The universe, the Goddess, allows free will in the context of the order of creation. Therefore, learning through experience is shown in all its glory and all its gory detail. You can most easily see that this is part of your nature, as well.

Now with all this going on, it does not mean that everyone in their cultures condoned what they did or how they did it. It only means that those who were here did those things. There were many more cultures and beings who have visited your world. Your planet's chronology is older than can be calculated and in this there have been many cultures, beings, civilizations and visitations. I am specifically omitting the names and cultures of these beings and the time frames. This is so you will not point a finger at good guys and bad guys. This is also so you will not measure time, figure out who was here when, and get locked into the judgment of being. That is not what this chronology imparts. Everything that has unfolded has brought you to this glorious moment in time. I am creating a thread for you to follow to see how and why your world has occurred in its fashion, and to describe more fully the energies of Alawashka for your highest joy.

In all this confusion of power struggles, rights of succession, wars, control, and plunder, which continued for a long period of time, certain beings began performing genetic experiments with the life forms on this planet. Each group who participated in these experiments had their reasons for doing so. Some of those reasons seemed very "altruistic" at the time. Most often, they really were experiments. An experiment is a group of actions taken to observe what occurs. This is then monitored. Sometimes the experiments are altered to produce specifically desired results. There was much of this going on. So while one group is noted historically for the creation of humans as you are today, they are not the only group who was involved. Humans were not the only recipients of genetic alteration. Experiments on animal and plant life were also undertaken.

The chronology of your world is infinitely rich and varied. Time is not a constant linear experience. Many stories concerning the galactic beings, the creator gods and the like, overlap in time. What may appear to predate the human recreation, may have followed it. The Lyrans may have been here first, the Sirians next, and the Annunaki next. The Pleiadians may have come to Earth before the Sirians or after the Annunaki, or perhaps there was a coexistence.

Following this specific chronological focus unravels the past to reveal your heritage. Through this unraveling you access the optimal ways of accelerating into your highest spirit. You can then begin to understand the meaning and import of the language of Alawashka for your world at this moment in time.

Those doing the main thrust of experiments came to find a wealth of resources to help their home world. They wanted workers to mine the gems and gold. This planet has many unique things. Beauty, minerals and Earth's unique energy are the most specific resources. There were also those on this planet who wanted to mine the emotions of the humans and began experiments to those ends.

Mining emotions means something very specific. Each emotion has a frequency. By exciting a specific frequency one can feel that energy. Just as you can feel the energy in a room when something upsetting has happened, so too, can other races of beings. These races not only created genetic experiments to aid in their personal opportunity, they did so to experience the frequencies created when emotions were elicited from the humans. They could actually experience and feed off of these energies. They didn't have experiences of emotion. Emotion is also an energy, and energy is a food. By eliciting the strongest emotional energy they could use, some beings could feed themselves. They could boost their personal energy by feeding off the emotional energy of the humans.

The easiest energy to elicit is fear. Since they did not experience emotion, fear was used as a power source. It is not a particularly high energy frequency, but it certainly works. They had no regard for the outcome of the experiments, save that they would be successful. These beings had no personal regard or thought for the humans or of the possible ramifications of their work. They just did the experiments because they could. They had the ability to do it.

The Lyran bond with this planet and Her life forms created a sense of guardianship among them and they stayed as long as they could. They were very much aware of the experimentation on humans. They knew the intent and purpose of these experiments, and they most certainly did not agree.

There was also a very covert experiment going on which had to do with galactic power. Some of these beings who were spearheading the genetic experimentation on Earth beings were also involved in a very secret experiment to gain power in their own world. They had visions of power beyond this galaxy. Even in that group, only one being was really working out the scheme. This scheme, which unfolded in genetic experimentation, was to create a super being out of their gene pool, the Earth gene pool and a galactic pool of genetic materials.

In this sector of the galaxy there was a great deal of inattention and trust. You may now think of it as naive trust and blind faith in the nature of being, but the inherent understanding was in the nature of greatness and evolution of all beings. It was an inner knowing that all beings everywhere are destined to evolution, higher frequency and blessed expression. That is true. Yet the pathway to this greater expression is sometimes paved with great turmoil, subjugation and greed.

At the head of this select group of scientists was a being that you refer to as a god. He was orchestrating an experiment to create a new galactic race in his image of perfection, and who would easily rule this sector of the galaxy. He gathered two other beings around him who were supremely gifted in genetics, energy manipulation and creation. They collected genetic and energetic materials from cultures all over this section of the galaxy, under a rouse to experiment with the specific strains of material to their greater understanding.

Even the brilliant female scientist working with him had no idea of the god's true intentions until it was much too late, and she was much too involved and curious. The strains of material were gathered and a goddess was selected for insemination. Now this could not be just any female of their race, but one of noble birth and heritage, one who could place her son upon a throne.

This great and ancient goddess had no idea what was going on. She knew that she was to be inseminated to carry the seed of a great one into the world. Her reward would be honor, power and wealth. Now, to do these experiments, one would have to choose a goddess who would find those things very tempting. She found them tantalizing and immediately volunteered. Her assumption was that it was the semen of a brother or the great ruler of her world. Little did she know that this seed was a blend of genetic materials from all over the galaxy. Each portion of this blend was chosen for specific traits, like strength, intelligence, cunning, passion, etc. Of course, they were chosen by this god for the things he decided were the best attributes. Our beautiful, unwitting goddess was about to be inseminated.

THE COUNCIL AND THEIR DECISION
The Response of the Lyrans and Anshara

At this particular time in chronology, there were governing councils who would oversee the goings on in many areas of the galaxy and the universe and meet to decide certain eventualities. The Council is a collection of very high frequency beings who attend to the matters of the universe to help the full expression and evolution of all beings. Through their all-inclusive focus they are aware of what is transpiring. They are a specific body of individually focused beings who have the full capacity to be directly aware of occurrences in a very vast area. They are also a decision making body. Their process can be viewed as one of discussion and decision through a full consensus. Everyone on the council must agree in the decision and in the suggested action. The foundation of their decisions was one of noninterference. This does not mean no action or no discussion. It means that their premise is not to alter the course of events unfolding or to avert the development and lessons of any and all cultures and beings. Free choice and free determination were key. The decisions for specific punitive actions would be the responsibility of the home culture, the culture of those engaging in an action that would come to the attention of the Council.

The Council is concerned with the universal principle of being. You call them the laws of nature. This is actually much more complex than you can imagine. A principle is not a fixed process. These principles or laws are organized methods of interpretation concerning the nature of creation. Not all principles apply to all beings. In this part of the universe, the Council can actually decide which universal principles of creation, order, structure and form are the most appropriate avenues in which form may develop.

When all of this Earth chronology of galactic visitation and human experimentation was unfolding, the Council upheld certain laws. Their full agreement is to uphold those laws and allow the free will of all beings to express those principles as they see fit. We may indeed see a revision of the Council's principles of order in the next few years, given what has happened to your world. There is a great deal of urgency in this. All of the universe is synchronistic. What has occurred to you, in this seemingly small part of the universe, is of great importance to all life. The principles of creation, the order in which creation unfolds, may need some revision, which is the responsibility of the Council. They respond to the expression of creation and organize its order of unfolding for its greater and higher expression.

The Council was aware of these events on Earth. They had been watching many of the situations on Earth and had not deemed it necessary to intervene in any way. They were monitoring. Some of the Council were more concerned than others, but it was agreed to continue to monitor. The Lyrans took the initiative to petition the Council to intervene. The Council debated endlessly and could not decide whether to intervene. The noninterference issue had almost all of them stuck. After all, the order of creation was being upheld, and the expression of creation and evolution was occurring in those specified parameters. In effect, there was nothing that should be done, since all was progressing within the agreed upon order and structure. It does not mean that the Council was uncaring, unconcerned or even aloof. They were acting within their powers to act, and not beyond them. While this has had seemingly dire consequences for you in certain respects, in other respects, the Council is one of the few groups who honor their specific stance in the universe, and do not generally overstep that specification. That is why they are on the Council.

There was one being on the Council who was not stuck in this dilemma. This being was outraged. This being wishes to be called Anshara. Anshara could see the fullness of the actions of those experimenting. He pleaded with the Council to stop the actions that were taking place. He could see that the experiments would have many ramifications due to the intent of the beings experimenting. The "scientists" involved in one of these earthly experiments were working to create a strain of humans who would have no connection to the Divine energies of the Goddess of the universe, and would be fully limited in their growth and development. He was outraged. The Council defeated his many pleas.

The Lyrans were aware of the Council's decision and began to actively infuse or align the energies of the humans with the language of Alawashka. Alawashka is a healing language. It creates a resonance within each person to align with the highest energies they can hold. This action was done to help keep the flames of creation alive in the humans. It was done so they would remember that they were Divine beings within the universe. While this was an infraction of the Council's decision, the Lyrans knew that since the Council would not intervene in this situation, they would not prevent any actions taken by the Lyrans. The Council would continue to monitor the unfolding events as they had decided. If the Council could not intervene, the Lyrans could then engage in the manner they felt was best. If the Council could not stop the experiments because of the focus and responsibility of their guidelines, then this also meant the Lyrans could continue or advance their workings because it was not deemed a full infraction of galactic order or principle.

Creating the greater opening for Alawashka within humans was a very subtle act to counter the genetic and energetic experiments that worked to separate the energy of the humans. This separation experiment, which was coming along nicely, was a very unique idea for controlling the population. The experiments created such a specific focus that the unique link all life forms had on this planet was severed.

Now, in non-judgmental terms, this could be considered a natural evolution of theory. The scientists prized their abilities to engage in a highly defined focus while connecting to the greater All. So, to continue creation experiments along this line is not an extreme deviation from the natural thrust. The deviation comes from using this focus as a controlling mechanism creating isolation, confusion and fear. They did know that this would be the outcome. This was the main objection that the Lyrans, Anshara and some others had to these experiments. To create beings that were permanently separated from the Divine by genetic and energetic creation was the worst thing they could imagine.

Anshara took an initiative that would isolate him from the Council. Anshara secretly tampered with the genetic materials being used in the experiment so the experiment could not be 100% effective. As genetic materials were being collected for the experiment, Anshara added a specific strain of coding to the mix which could and would hold some of the connection to the Divine in place. This action would make the experiment ninety percent effective, remain fully undetected, and leave a ten percent opening for the connection to unfold. It is interesting to note that your Earth scientists speculate that only ten percent of your brain is actually engaged in your life. They speculate that ninety percent of your capabilities remains to be explored. Is this ninety percent unused capability the area that shows where the experimentations were highly successful? Is that ten percent opening the area left active by Anshara in his secret tampering with the galactic experiment?

Anshara is not in your direct line of ancestry and is a very ancient being. His place on the Council was esteemed. His ability to see the future consequences of these alterations extended throughout time. Anshara is not held by time. He can follow and assess any number of possible, probable and likely futures. In his extensive search of all deviations in the results of the experiments, through the chronology of time, he could not find one situation that would put him at ease. Each situation, played out in its probable direction, would result in fear and isolation for humanity. Now, Anshara does not experience emotions in ways that humans do. When I mention that he was outraged or upset, it is a resonance that is in extreme discord with his nature. What you would describe as a negative emotion, he would feel as a profound energetic dissidence. His decision created conflict within him, but his greater conflict was knowing the inevitable effects of the experiments. This dynamic energetic tension, created by his position on the Council and his full understanding of the future, forced him into an irrevocable decision.

He fully understood the ramifications of his actions, but the part he played gave the Lyrans the opportunity to create the frequency for humans to hold without its being discovered. He created the opening so the Lyrans and other beings working to help the humans keep their energetic connection to the All, to their possible evolution, would have the greatest chance of success without detection. He was still a member of the Council, but the opinions of those on the Council was that he was not to be trusted to uphold their full intent. He was isolated from the Council at that time, and stories of his actions were circulated among his peers.

Now while all this was being debated in the Council, Anshara was very much aware of the secret experiments going on to create a super being. The Lyrans and the Council were not aware of this particular event while it was unfolding. Anshara was. Since the debates for the sake of the Earth beings were deemed untouchable, he knew very well that the experiments for the new child would gain even less consideration. The "super child soup" was being perfected at the very time the human experiments were being conducted. This particular experiment was to have even more profound effects, because not only would this new child be a ruler on Earth, but a created ruler intended to take power in the galaxy and expand the rule of the gods, specifically creating a new dynasty from god the orchestrator and goddess the mother.

The intention of this particular strain of material was similar to the human experiment in that the new child was to be controlled by the god orchestrator to his ends. Anshara read the frequencies of this being quite well, and acted according to his assessment. He added something else to the "super child soup." He added a portion of his own awareness. This would not be considered genetic materials, but rather a very minute energetic infusion, if you like, a particular electrical charge. Again, his intention was to create an opening for awareness. It did not generate the awareness, but create the possibility that it would or could unfold.

The goddess was inseminated and to the delight of the three, this first insemination took hold. Yet, from the very beginning there were problems. This was a difficult pregnancy. There was great physical pain and discomfort. There were unusual symptoms. This was all due to the enormous variation in the genetic material, and our goddess was not even remotely aware of what she was carrying. She was dreaming of a beautiful little boy child who would be radiant and gifted and rule with great majesty. What she was carrying gave her pain and illness and was carried months longer than was usual or even anticipated.

The birthing was painful and she required great medical skill and attention to see her through it. When at last the child was delivered and placed into her arms, she wept bitter tears. This was not the perfect boy child of her dreams. This child was a blend of beings, whose features were coarse and alien. As she gazed into her child's eyes, searching for understanding and inwardly pleading for the meaning of this birth, cruel eyes stared back at her. A great pain and shiver ran through her. She believed she had carried an abomination into life. She was in duress and trauma and she fully rejected her child. Even the orchestrating god and the great scientist were shocked. This was not the being that they had thought to create. And for the god, whose intention was to rule behind the child, well, he already knew that his fate was sealed and that doom was in the air.

However, this did not stop him from working on the human experiments. He proceeded diligently, tried to forget his fiasco, and left the child to others to care for. This child grew to rule, but he also grew to despise his being and his heritage. There are many myths and stories which partially tell of his life, some of which are found in the Sumerian chronologies. Much of this story has never been told because the god and goddess wished this to remain hidden. Their lives have evolved and they are no longer within the same expression of frequency. Yet, this child grew to destroy nations and loath humans, while creating great temples in his own name. He irradiated the planet without concern. His hatred was greater than anyone could have imagined. His vendetta against his mother impelled him to try to purge her from this planet and kill all who loved her. He endeavored to take control of every tool, every skill and every wisdom for his rule and control.

While he is not the focus of this chronology, he is within your myths and histories, although grossly miswritten to protect the guilty. I include this concurrent event in the chronology of the human experiment to give you a suggestion of the pathways that may unfold when experimentation is undertaken with mal-intent.

At the same time as the birth of the super child, the human experiments were completed. The humans, for the first time, began to feel alone. They could no longer feel their connection to all beings on this planet. They could no longer sense their connection to the Divine, the Goddess, the All. The humans were manipulated into their isolation by outside forces. It was not their natural way to feel alone and separate. This created fear in a highly elevated state. Fear was generally a response to an outside force. Now fear was an inner emotion, and it occurred because of their experience of limitation and separation from everything.

Humans were farmed and created. Existing humans were altered. New humans were created by artificial means and by means of artificial insemination, not so dissimilar to your own procedures. Some of the racial coding was mixed. Some of it was newly developed. Some of the galactic females were inseminated with the DNA of the human males. Their births were painful. The beings, part human, part galactic were difficult for these women to embrace as their own. The galactic females who participated in this experiment were not informed as to the nature of the experiment or the toll it would take on their energies and their physical bodies. The shock and confusion that occurred was almost beyond their endurance. The 'children' of this strain were considered demigods, and this was supposedly an honored gift from the galactic women to their race. It was very good propaganda to help get healthy stock for the experiments. Certain galactic women of royal blood, of rulership class, were specially chosen for this honor. In their pampered, naive belief that they were helping their own race, they agreed.

Many of your Sumerian, Egyptian and Biblical myths elude to these events. The myths were specifically rewritten to enhance the stories in their best light, which is something all of you are familiar with through your own media's interpretations of events. The victors always write history that extol themselves. The media creates stories in the light they wish to present. This time in your chronology was the foundation of what you experience in your world today. Your media is a manipulation of your minds and a distraction. A few truths are brought forth to cover a multitude of lies. Drama is created to manipulate the people and distract all of you from the specific events that are working under the surface of those much publicized events.

The media is distracting you from the truth in carefully choreographed dramas that will engage you in that thought. The truth is that you are all Divine beings. You are no less than the very gods who have "created" you. Yet, if you view the media and experience your world through the portions of your mind that have been tampered with, all you will see is the limitation, the lack of control of your minds and your bodies, the hierarchy of others and your small place in it all.

All you will see is your isolation from the Divine and your powerlessness. Well, this is very effective for keeping you in your place. Your computer wizards would be in awe of this form of programming.

Human women were continually kept pregnant. New ways of manipulating the reproductive cycle of humans were developed so that women could be continually inseminated and birth the workers that were required. These alterations were performed on women who were genetically fully human, of the Earth. When certain women were able to be fertile numerous times and birth the particular strains of beings that were most beneficial to the galactic scientists, then a new series of experiments ensued. The gods procreated with the female humans. Human males also had experimentations and alteration, but the galactic scientists found that the females of their own galactic race soon recognized the extreme burden of birthing this new form, and refused to participate. So while the males were directly altered as well, the females of Earth had the greater hardship of birthing their own altered race.

This experiment created a very new situation on this planet. The humans were now in a position to be controlled. Those who were the first to undergo the experiments were severed from the Universal All. Those who were born of the experiments were also severed from the All. They could no longer access their Divine selves in the ways they were used to. They could no longer communicate with the other beings and life forms of this planet. They could no longer find food in the ways they once did. They could no longer navigate. They could no longer remember in the ways natural to them. They were, in effect, isolated from their own selves. The races of outsider beings who were living here created a limitation within the humans so they could be controlled. And they were. The humans worked to mine things, to raise crops, to generate the fear food which could be ingested by certain beings and to do tasks the others did not wish to do. This is also part of your heritage. While you carry the seeds, the codes of divinity within, you carry this separation as well.

As chronology continued, the humans became closer to the ruler races. They were good, efficient slaves. Those beings who provided the food, the shelter, the leadership were looked upon for the only connection the humans could sense. The ruler race was firm, directed, strong and powerful. They had abilities the humans did not have. This was the only sense of strength that the humans could hold onto, because the inner connection was gone. They started to emulate the ruler races. They learned and spoke the cultural languages of the other beings. They learned to view the world as outside of themselves. Some humans became more proficient at certain tasks, and began to rule over those who were less proficient. They were in effect, used as management. They could help the galactic beings rule over and control the other humans. They began taking on leadership roles in a very limited fashion. They would direct the mining, organize the people for farming and participate in the religious rituals of the galactic invaders, as if it were their own natural expression.

This was not how it was before the experiments. Before the experiments everyone was honored for their own gifts. The society was very communal and caring. Leaders were not chosen to rule the whole group of individuals. Each communed with divinity and the path to take was clear. At times one person was relied upon for a particular skill, but once that person had guided the others, then that same person was back to being one of the community. All people could connect with the Divine energies of the planet and the animal and plant beings. All people could find their food and avert the Earth movements. Each was an individual, but with such a strong connection to the whole that they did not need to assert individuality. Yes, they were considered primitive. They had simple but effective tools. They had gentle ways of walking on the Earth. They knew the power spots for healing and energy, and they honored their personal passage into the other realms which you call death. They even chose specific plants and animals to eat to merge with the wisdom within each food. They chose places to live that were not only based on whether food sources were plentiful, but also where the energy was perfect for their being and gentle evolution. With the alteration of genetic coding, none of this could be relied upon as an inherent part of their being. It was, in effect, removed.

Now that they acquired some of the genetic codes of the very races who were experimenting upon them, they were emulating some of their behavior. This was naturally seen as a great sign by the races, and it was encouraged behavior. The personality traits of the galactic races held some very interesting and potent possibilities, but they were shut down. Those portions that were accessible were not what you might consider traits to emulate. There was a great selfishness and fear within the galactic visitors and their coding. There was a disregard for all life, except for the select groups deemed fit. There were great power struggles. Humanity didn't have these before, but with the expertise of the genetic scientists, you certainly did afterwards. With all of these new attributes, all they had to do was affect the isolation and generate fear, and off you went in the direction of their choosing. Unfortunately, you are still responding to those very same suggestions in the very same manner.

THE EXPERIMENTS
The Influences of Anshara and the Lyrans

This system of control through separation and fear continues to this day on your planet. Your races are divided. Your money is controlled by a few. Your governments are working to separate you all, in order that they may have the money and the power. The media distorts messages and infuses useless information to entertain you and divert your connection to each other and to the Divine. There are groups that are infusing this energy and manipulating those that you might assume are manipulating you. So some of those in your government who seem to be the ones that are manipulating you into terrible acts of aggression and undermining your financial solvency, are also being manipulated by forces of highly trained alchemists who are working their charms on them. These alchemical scientists are, in turn, manipulated by the creator gods. It is not always a conscious event employed by the religions, media or the government. Of course, sometimes it is very conscious.

There are those who are undermining all the divinity within you. They are indeed in your governments, your media and your religions. They are also very involved with all types of business and science. And, they are manipulated by the fear and isolation that seeks control as a panacea for the separation from the Divine, especially from the Goddess. They want this control so badly, and are so separated from their own divinity, that this is all they can do. This is in your genetic makeup and in your energetic access. This is just how it is working. There is no judgment or condemnation in this.

In every moment there is always the opportunity for growth, evolution and connection with the Divine. Many of the beings who came here and did all this have evolved into splendid energies. It is through their very actions that they saw the nature of control and have overcome this pattern. They have been able to discern the nature and impetus of their actions and release the patterns that were controlling them. There have been many alliances and galactic healings because of your past. These have been quite profound.

Those on the Council, who once repudiated Anshara, have had reconciliations with him. The highest levels of the breaches caused by these events on your world have been healed and sealed. Many of the beings who enacted these events have reached higher levels of expression and experience. This whole aspect of your chronology has set new precedents into the works. Many original breaches of being have been healed. This has opened a new level of expression for everyone, every being in the universal wholeness.

I say this just for you to notice and understand some of the patterns you are living within. When you discern the patterns that are moving you away from your celebration of divinity, when you can see the patterns within you that are creating fear and separation from the greatest blessings of life, you will be able to discern the outer triggers that elicit these from your being. You will then seize every moment for your highest growth and evolution.

You cannot give up what you have not owned. This means that you cannot give up your fears, isolation, and need for control, if you do not fully recognize that these are working within you. They are driving you. When you see them and you can feel how they are working toward your inner isolation, then you can release them. You can notice the games and manipulations and those circumstances that trigger you into anger, or depression (suppressed anger), or fear or increase your sense of isolation. You can watch it, connect with the Divine which is All, and let it go. This is transformation and evolution.

Within the earliest portion of this time frame, the Lyrans were still present. They had found an access to the humans that could not be detected by the others. The Lyrans knew that any altering of the experiment would be detected. They could not physically alter any of the genetic codes, because that would be discovered. So Anshara created an access within the human form that could not be readily detected and the Lyrans worked to infuse this access with Alawashka. The brilliance of Anshara was that he created space, a concealed absence of anything distinguishable within the DNA experiment. This access can be viewed as an opening. Nothing was inserted, nothing was changed that could be detected. He created a space, an energetic holding system, which is a vessel for the Goddess within each person. It is a container for the Divine connection, which has memory of the All within all. It is a vessel which can be activated, yet before it is activated, it cannot be detected or discovered. This opening was so incredibly subtle that none of the scientists could even sense that it was there.

Anshara had no intention of altering humanity. He wanted preservation of the Divinity in and of humanity. Understanding his integrity in this allows you to know him. He created the opening, the containment of divinity within humanity, so the inherent connection could be preserved. This enabled the Lyrans to reinforce the memories of Alawashka within humanity. It also provided a place to infuse Alawashka into those who were more severely altered.

The Lyrans had the task of infusing this energetic holding system with the essence of Divine connection. By working with Alawashka, the Lyrans were able to establish an undetectable aspect of Divine blessing within humanity. The language of Alawashka is not an implant. It does not alter genetic coding nor create any measurable changes. This aspect was crucial. The scientists were fully capable of monitoring every change in the human physiology. Each experiment was carefully supervised. Any changes would certainly be noticed. Any perceived failures in their mission would be rectified. The Lyrans had to find the most effective strategy for Alawashka's successful introduction.

Very subtle contacts with specific humans were made. The Lyrans were looking for the most advantageous opening. They found that during women's menstrual cycles and the full cycle of embodying the seed of life, the bond of creation, the presence of the Goddess could not be controlled or eliminated. During pregnancy, the inner bond of mother, child and the Divine, could not be controlled. In the cycles of women, the pull of the Divine was the strongest. Women might be monitored for the health of their children, but certainly not for their connection to the Goddess or to Gaia. It is interesting to note how the blood of women was their most powerful access to the Divine. That connection, that rich blood, was only from the women. It was at that time of bleeding and in the rhythm of creating life, that the opening could be greatly accessed. This was more efficient for the Lyrans than monitoring the men, who would open and close at whim. The women had a clear cycle of opening to divinity. This had always been so, even before the experiments. With the increase in the frequency of fertility, the access with women was a regulated event, just like the cycles of the moon. So, the Lyrans worked with the women.

Many of the women were engineering for breeding. More workers were needed and the women were kept pregnant as often as possible. The Lyrans started to teach the sacred language of Alawashka to the women. It was their only hope of holding the frequency of the Divine within the human race. Small ceremonies were created by linking interdimensionally. Alawashka was spoken. This was all done in secret. It was done in dreams and in inner journey work. The Lyrans triggered the energetic holding system and a great unfolding occurred. It was like tapping a beautiful flower and having it joyfully open to be pollinated.

Each woman wanted to hold Alawashka within. This was not done against her higher will. While under the controlling pattern of the scientists, a sacred link could not even be fathomed. During the menstrual cycles and during pregnancy, a woman's natural inclination was to open to the divinity of the Goddess. Women would feel the pull of the moon and open to Alawashka with great regularity. Those few women who were minutely aware of this difference knew to keep it hidden. They could feel the greater connection within them. However, most women were consciously oblivious to the call of the moon tides and revealed themselves to Alawashka in the safety of their dreams.

The Lyrans were concerned that this could create another experience of separation. Working more exclusively with the women could create another isolation pattern. They were concerned about this division. A division between men and women would have repercussions, especially because these would mimic the hostilities between the female and male creator gods. They did work with the men, but because the men had, on the whole, taken more completely to the experimentation, working with them was more difficult and much trickier. The Lyrans also knew that to not act, to leave the humans fully separated from the Divine at this time, would be to abandon them to isolation forever.

Many more events occurred on this planet. Beings came and went. Earth became a free-for-all for beings who did not honor the gifts She freely offered. The creator gods came for vacation and refueling, and then left. They continued to beef up their controls of the frequencies of the planet and create lock out systems so that humanity would not evolve and others could not come here. Their turmoil and hunger for control created systems dedicated to monitoring and regulating the human experience. Other races saw those who were coming here to plunder, and endeavored to change the situation. They added new codes to some humans. They worked to create more accessible frequencies to the planet. They brought different energy systems to help humanity and Gaia.

Intergalactic conflicts occurred. Wars among other races broke out. Some of these conflicts were fueled by the conflicts here. Some of the conflicts were an excuse to rekindle old conflicts that had existed in their own worlds.

While previously tentative relations were upheld with differing galactic cultures, the disagreements caused by the Earth's turmoil embroiled certain factions. Wars broke out on Earth. The authority given to some creator gods was the source of much jealousy among other creator gods. Power struggles between family members were the norm. Civil wars, wars of dominion and control were fought. The remaining Lyrans had no choice but to leave. They had given the gift of Alawashka to the Earth and worked with the humans to help keep the connection to the Divine open, even if it was only within the realm of possibilities, and not experienced as a direct source. The devastation on this planet threatened their existence. Their time on Earth was over and they left.

ALL ALONE WITH NO WHERE TO GO
The Human Equation

All of the conflicts, particularly those generated on Earth by those who had come to control it, also threatened the existence of the races in control. They were continually fighting and trying to destroy each other for rulership of Earth and positions of greatest authority. They blasted this planet with radiation. They helped create natural disasters as a means of controling the humans and as a means of power over each other. Portions of this planet were ravaged. Waters were dried up or polluted. Great fertile valleys were barren. This situation got so intense and so devastating for the ecology of Terra that within time, the galactic rulers too, left the planet. This was not their home, it was their vacation land. They had a permanent stop in their planetary sojourn, and Earth was it. They did not intend to live here forever. They had their own world. They only wanted a piece of the galaxy to dominate and control, and then they would leave again. Once they started wreaking havoc here, it was a good time to leave. They had escalated a series of events they could not possibly manage. Party's over, time to leave, so to speak. They had mined the gold, fought many battles, experimented to the fullest extent, had enough fun for now, and were on their way. This is not the culture of beings who stay after the party and help clean up the mess.

The humans were left alone. With their connection to the Divine severed, held in containment as a remote

75

evolutionary possibility, the humans were left in isolation, confusion and fear. They were left alone in a world of great destruction. Food was scarce. The natural flow of rivers was changed. The gentle balance of this beautiful planet was altered. Their aloneness was even greater, now that they had no one to rule over them. They had looked toward the galactic races for care and direction. They had worshipped them. The creators had great powers. They were the source of all good things. Indeed they were. With the connection to divinity and Gaia severed, how could humans find food, shelter and spiritual unity? The gods did this for them. They were the gods and the rulers. They gave them all the food, taught them agriculture and warfare, and were their source of spirit and all good things. The gods were gone. Now the people were abandoned. They were left to themselves.

Naturally, the men who had been encouraged to rule over the others in managerial positions took their places as full rulers. Some of them had worked in the temples of their rulers. Some of them had directed working facilities. Some of them farmed the food for the ruler gods. Some of them had military experience. They took the place of the departed races and became the rulers of the human populations. Someone had to tell humanity what to do, and these men were the most qualified, especially in respect to the positions they held when the gods were on the planet. They were those chosen by the gods to manage, now they would assume the roles of rulership.

The people began to travel. They scattered across the Earth in search of better food, water and safer places to live. While some groups remained close to the civilizations that were still standing, others were led into unknown lands. There was no group consensus of direction and they followed their new leaders into different parts of the planet. They adopted the languages of the races of galactic beings who had once ruled them, and they wandered the lands.

Some people stayed in the lands of the gods. They stayed in Sumeria, Egypt, and the greater Nile area. Their civilizations grew to some extent, yet when you look at the slow degeneration of the structures built after the time of the gods, you will see that much of it could not be maintained in the same manner. The rituals of the temples of the gods continued. Now the human rulers were the gods. They were the Divine connection of the people. They did not have the technologies of creation, of weather manipulation, of interplanetary travel, of genetics, and of all manner of magical skills of their gods. They were similar in personality as those galactic beings who had altered their genes and created the human as it is today. They were progeny of the gods in certain respects. They controlled the rituals, the harvests, the warriors, and carried on in the manner of their god creators.

Initially, all aspects of life carried on as before with hopes of pleasing the galactic creator gods. They wanted to find favor with the galactic beings who left them, so that they would return and bring joy and bounty with them. The gods had promised their return, and these celebrations would insure it.

Other civilizations sprung in different areas and the population of humanity spread. They, too, followed in the footsteps of the gods. They created civilizations and worshipped in the ways they were taught. I shall say that the further away from the structures of the Nile civilizations they traveled, the less control was within their civilization. This is a general statement. You will find that indigenous cultures have stronger memories of the planet than those people within the cities. This is because it is so much easier to control and manipulate humans who are closer to the civilized areas. When you are living in greater concentration, each event or energy that is beamed to you is excited by the population, carried quickly through the energy field and is increased. Therefore, control and manipulation of thought, response and memory can be more easily accomplished in more metropolitan areas.

Survival in the city relies on shutting down the relationship to all people and narrowing your energy field. This shuts out the communion with the All quite effectively.

This shut-off valve generates an energy build up with no outlet and so it affirms personal isolation, and allows control from the outside to be thoroughly welcomed. In effect, congested areas of population in a city structure begs for authority to intervene in all matters, including spirit.

In a smaller culture, a situation is nearly immediately handled by the group or by those involved. In the larger population areas, you rely on others to handle this for you. You are controlled by their response, which is controlled by the leaders' response, which is controlled by the system that created the isolation in the first place. The further away from the centralized control of religion, commerce and government, the louder the pulse of Terra becomes. The louder Her pulse, the more connected you are with Her and with your own divinity.

This does not mean that you all have to move out into the country. I show you this for a greater understanding of how the civilizations grew and how the controls were expedited. Understanding how this has grown, how the longing for outside management has grown, gives you the potential of calling your own spiritual relationship back into play. You don't have to relocate to claim this connection. Know that it is there, and the systems will have less impact.

When you fully realize the gods are not going to save you, and they never did save you, you will be in greater access to your own divinity. The gods will never save you, because they never intended to save you. They didn't create you with the joy of divinity and celebration of spiritual evolution. They created you for control. They are the ones who created the isolation you are working to overcome.

There are intergalactic beings who worked with you, and did not require worship. They were here before the creator gods. They were here after the creator gods. They placed new energy grids within the Earth to help stabilize it. They brought new teachings to help you break some of these patterns. They created interdimensional gateways in ancient sites to infuse you and the planet with more light. They have helped realign some of the energies of this planet. They worked with humans to give them access to the higher dimensions of being. They, too, altered your being. Some of these travelers have worked with the existing patterns from Anshara and the Lyrans. Others developed new patterns and codings to help you.

There are so many beings who have come to work with you. To list them all would still not give you the full understanding that you are choosing this life and path. Through your choices you have the opportunity to bring all of the wisdom and consciousness to this planet in this portion of time.

There have been beings all along who, like Anshara and the Lyrans, have created openings. They have created openings, energy balancing, moved frequency points, stabilized solar activity, diffused dramatic Earth change and galaxy change activities. An amazing amount of work from blessed beings has been focused to bring your full awakening to fruition. This is not only your past. It is a relationship that continues to this day.

Many beings from this past that I describe have continued to evolve. They understand what their participation has delivered, and they know their responsibilities for their actions. Through their dedication to humanity, they have worked for endless ages to bring greater light, energy and vision to you and your world. They have all worked with Gaia and worked with humans, animals, plant life and the elemental world. They continue to come to your aid, but coming to your aid is very different than saving you. When you realize that you are not isolated from the Goddess, you will create the harmony and miracles of joy in every breath you take. You will realize that you have the supreme power to give your attention to the evolution of your world and the spiritual grace of your being. You are safe. You are always safe within the Goddess. You are that which is the All.

THE ALAWASHKA SECRET
Seed Memories

No matter where the cultures traveled, no matter how the civilizations developed, inside each individual was the seed of Alawashka. Alawashka, the seed of memory, the seed of connection to the Divine, is always carried within. Anshara made sure that the fertile ground was ever present and pure. The Lyrans planted this elegant and beautiful seed. Within each being the discretely hidden opening for connection, frequency and evolution remained. In certain places the humans began to connect again. The women remembered the language. They did not remember all of it, but they remembered portions of it. In the fleeting memories of dreams and insights they pieced together some of the words and some of the rituals taught to them by the Lyrans when they were in journey or dream state. They created their own ceremonies and rituals to connect with the Divine. These few women came together to explore and to remember. They created teachings and rites to bring their memories and connection to the Goddess into a greater focus. They worked together to feel their relationship to the source. The men were always welcome and some of them did participate.

These were the pockets of new civilizations that sprang in many places on this planet. Many of these cultures were in remote areas, on islands, in forests, and in the mountains. They did not specifically emulate those galactic beings who had once ruled over them. Some of these cultures became communal again. The men and women were honored and appreciated for their gifts. The separation was still present, but they had formed a bridge to themselves and the Divine.

Other cultures were split. Some of them fully adopted the culture and religions of the galactic rulers. The galactic rulers had created propaganda against women because women were not ruled so easily. On their home planet, women had ruling capacities, but did not necessarily employ those facets of life. Their power was understood, but never exercised. The nature of this culture was that if a power or right was not employed, it did not exist. When this race came to Earth and through the exploration of their powers, some of these women exercised their rights and influence as rulers. By the nature of their home cultures, rights of succession and rulership had birth and family lineage. Specific females here, also had these rights and were exercising them to rule, create cities and religious rites in their own fashion. This created even more discord as family members took sides on who ruled which lands, whether the experiments on humans were ethical, who received greater benefits and power and the like.

Several of the women formed cities and armies and opposed the rulers they disagreed with, who always happened to be male. The males were those who exercised their rulership powers in that culture. Expert propaganda was circulated against any galactic female asserting power and many battles and wars were fought. The conflicts were power struggles for the right to rule this whole planet and everyone on it, in whatever manner seemed fit to the one in charge. When the females had too much power, chronology, in a "his-storical" fashion, was rewritten to show the females in their worst light. All the creator gods here were working toward control of the Earth. None of them were high glorious beings who bestowed great blessings and evolution for all here on Earth. Some of them were decidedly more domination oriented, and disseminated the most efficient propaganda against their "enemies."

The first "enemies" of the new rulers were the females, and then it was anyone opposed to them. They set themselves up as gods, to be worshipped obeyed and to control as much of the Earth and her population as possible. The Goddess was relegated to a lowly position. She became an afterthought, both in the minds of the creator gods, and later in the minds of the humans. It was known that this planet and Divine creation was female. To assume and keep control, the Goddess and the female were set up to be despised. This propaganda was also circulated to the humans. Because they were part of the property of this planet, and because of the separation experiments, they would follow leaders against the females in simple childlike allegiance. Women were portrayed as devious, manipulative, horrible creatures that would surely cause great trouble and ruin for all people. This is the beginning of the separation of male and female into polarity on your world.

Some of the wandering human populations fully embraced the propaganda that women were devious, lower, subversive beings who should be treated with disdain and controlled at all costs. They worshipped the male gods of the galactic races and subjugated women in their societies. Man ruled. He took the distorted view that was given him by the galactic rulers as a truth and acted accordingly. This was an emulation of the galactic rulers who were on this planet and not of their whole culture. The male was considered supreme. With this came all the personality traits of the creator gods. The creator gods thought that male energy was better, stronger and more powerful, based on their naive and adolescent maturity. This was what they brought forth into the world of humans. This was all that humanity had to believe in because this was what the galactic gods believed. It was also what was left, because the true connection to the Divine All, which celebrates all Her creations, was separated through the success of the experiments.

In some newly developing cultures, the men worshipped the gods of the rulers and the women worshipped the Goddess, the divinity they felt through Alawashka. These women held onto the language the longest. They were always threatened with outside forces who wished to control the energies. These cultures also eventually became male dominated, because of their admiration of the ruler races, the influence of other human cultures, and because of the inherent experimental change that saw control as the only way to overcome fear and isolation.

As a result, the women's rituals and celebrations became secret. It appeared that the more secretive the women were about their Divine relationships with Gaia and the Goddess, the longer they could survive in the world. They held onto their inner language, Alawashka, as best they could, and participated in their communities as they were needed. They held secret ceremonies and rituals. They worked with Alawashka in healings and initiations. They worked with the lunar and fertility cycles of women. They taught their female children and held onto the grace of the Goddess in every way possible.

Some of these women left the male dominated societies and created their own cultures. They left mixed society in order to remember the language and hold the connection. They created all-female societies and female-led societies where the Goddess could be freely honored and celebrated. They created a separation from the men in order to bring forth the energies in the ways they remembered. They remembered the language infused within their dreams. They remembered parts of the secret rituals and journeys the Lyrans had taught. They remembered the sacred times of the menses and pregnancy when the bonds were the strongest. The isolation was still present, but memories and energies flowed within them. There are archeological remains of this connection all over the planet. There are famous cultures who, even in the excavations of their artifacts and even through the misinterpretations of the "noted" archeologists, are clearly balanced, harmonious and productive societies of women.

The amazing cleverness and effectiveness of the Lyran and Anshara agreement is to be noted. They could not have foreseen that the galactic creator gods would discriminate against the women. This was not apparent from the initial circumstances. Those rulers maligned the women of their culture only to gain greater power and control. They continued to write many horrible stories about the cruelties of the female goddesses. This occurred not only on their initial visit, but in their subsequent visits to Earth as well. The great success of the creativity of the Lyrans and Anshara is revealed and magnified by these events. Pushing women further and further away from the controlling center of civilization enabled the women to keep their inner signals cleaner. Since they were not esteemed within the core of their cultures and their societies, the spiritual relationship that was within all people was heightened in the women. It fused a female underground culture which carried Alawashka and the Goddess deep inside while their practices remained hidden from the general population and the eyes of the galactic control.

Terra is a Goddess. She helped the women remember their divinity. She would continually trigger the women in their monthly cycle and in their gestation cycle. Terra held Alawashka within Her, and linked with the women in their menses cycles and resonated with Alawashka. It was a reciprocal beaming network. The women would resonate with their blood times and this would trigger the memories of Alawashka within. Gaia Terra would beam Alawashka within the lunar cycles and the women and Terra would resonate together. They would feel the connection of the Goddess, of their true divinity. The many taboos of female blood are clues to all women of the powers and memories held within your blood.

It is important to know and understand that the woman's cycle is not ended with menopause. The cycle of three is yet present. The girl child contains the essence and the codes of the blood, yet she has not begun to bleed. The memories and the opening of Alawashka and the Goddess are within her. She is not separated because she has not experienced the bleeding times. She is priming herself to be able to hold the infusion of energies.

The woman who bleeds has the activation. She is the testament. She is the vessel of the sacrament. Her blood shows the codings and the memories for all. This is most sacred, and most visible. Her blood is fertile and rich. Women's rituals of today are remembering this potency. They are blessing the land and their bodies with the sanctity and power of their blood.

Many women, now, are in their third stage. As the memory of the power of menstrual blood returns and is more readily available, these women feel that they have missed their sacred times. There is longing in their hearts for the power of the blood. I say to you, dear crones, that you have the power of the blood within. The maiden is the power of the blood yet to be revealed. The mother is the power of the blood revealed. The crone is the power of the blood of infused revelation. This is the power of knowing. The power of possibility is the female child. The power of the actualization is the mother. The power of the full cycle in-keeping is the crone.

The further away from the controlling civilizations the women were, the stronger they felt the pull toward the Goddess. Yet, the propaganda of the creator gods and the acting agents now in rulership positions drove the women into greater and greater secrecy. This actually kept Alawashka and the Goddess more alive in their souls. The more the women were isolated from the men, the more their opportunities to remember pressed forward.

This is not a road for you to follow. I am not suggesting that women leave their men and try to uncover these signals now. That time is over. Your time is to uncover divinity within yourselves and stop looking for it in other places.

The gateways to the other expressions of divinity only seem to be located outside of yourselves. There are many beings who have a different access who can help you understand the gateways and dimensions. Know that the keys to these gateways are within your own being.

It is not true that "you can't get there from here." *Here* is the only place you can get *there* from. If you don't start from *here*, then there is no *there* to get to. In other words, the *there* that you want to get to, is *here*. You are the location.

All anyone can do for you is to tell you where to look and how to access it. Be skeptical if anyone or any being tells you they can take you there. How can they take you inside your own being? Inside your own being is where the highest dimensions and the universe unfolds for you.

You are all opening to this sublime energy. You are all moving into recognition of the Divine gateways, male and female alike. Men and women are both glorious beings of great spirit. The harsh divisions on your world are not your natural Divine expression. Your communion as beings celebrating life together has been altered to react in againstness and separation.

While to some it may look as though men are the perpetrators and women the victims, it is not so. Men's reactions, their fear, their need for power and control, may appear to be different. The triggers that affect civilization and humanity are the same for men as for women. Men and women were both separated from their original wholeness and communion. This separation enforces division, first from your innate divinity, then from each other. It insures a sense of otherness in every direction. This separation created the friction with society, family and the environment. The specific responses to this antagonistic friction are obvious.

Please know, there are no victims. Each of you have played many roles in many times to fully understand this experience in order to uplift it. Also know that the profound gift of this polarity is unyielding clarity. You can't avoid seeing this force of opposition that keeps you from each other, from relating powerfully to each other, to the Earth and to the Divine. You feel it; you see it. It is communicated to you from the news, from business, from your homes and from your relationships. It is inescapable and that is a profound gift in itself. If you can see it, then you have the power to dissolve it.

THE STRUCTURES OF CULTURE
Holding the Openings in the Face of Isolation

As chronology continued to unfold, humanity traveled and many diverse cultures arose. Most often historically recorded societies emulated the old rulers and built structures and cities and created ways of worship that emulated the old rulers. They developed their cultures patterned on the ways of the conquering races they knew. Stories and legends developed about the powers and gifts of these rulers. Within all the cultures was the isolation and fear resulting from the experiments. Hidden within the isolation was the seed of Alawashka.

Conquerors came and went. Cultures clashed with other cultures. The creator gods came back and left again. They stepped up their control of the human population, started other cultural centers and created some very efficient secret societies who would start to dominate the smaller cultures. Languages were changed and sometimes forbidden as means of control. Cultures were altered. And men rose up against women. It was an unfortunate but understandable circumstance.

The men had been programmed, in a way, to see women as other, as an aberration to the rule. They were also aware, and inwardly knew, that the women held the frequency of Alawashka within them. This factor could not be hidden from the creator gods for too long. They may not have understood how this all came about, how the women were still remotely in touch with their Divine nature, but it was beginning

89

to be quite evident. The women held Alawashka and the Divine connection the longest. They held the energies and created rituals to remember that relationship. This bond led them to greater understanding of the Divine. It led them to the herbs and healing plants to aid the sick and injured. It led them to greater community. It led them to inner knowing. It led them to understand the nature of love. It led them to a greater connection with the Goddess. It led them away from fear and isolation and away from manipulation and control.

This was viewed as a vile threat to the rulers. To be uncontrollable, to refuse to follow, even in the smallest way, was viewed as a threat to the whole community. The rulers were angry. The creator gods were angry and perplexed. While in pockets of certain cultures the women and Alawashka were protected, many other cultures began to purge the women's powers. The gods, the rulers and the secret societies began inquisitions against women. Women were not the only ones cited for this purging. Scientists, astrologers, spiritual leaders, artists, musicians, healers and Divine beings were also recognized as opponents to the gods. They were slated for extermination, exile and torture, or at least financial ruin.

Generally, social classes, governments and cultures who persecute thinking, creative persons, do so because they recognize a threat to their control. Those persecuted artists, scientists, healers, creative thinkers, indigenous cultures, visionaries, spiritual seekers and religious groups hold secrets of the Divine within.

Many times in your chronology when humanity's gifts were coming to the fore, to benefit the opening of thought and spirit, these gifts were rapidly curtailed. Artists whose visions were opening the cosmic codes by what they painted were persecuted, tortured or otherwise done away with by social pressure or propaganda. So too, were the great scientists, who actually saw the other dimensions of being, and plotted ways to travel beyond this dimension. They traveled in their hearts and with their minds and began to see the energetic control mechanisms placed around your world. Well, what would you do if your whole network of control could be seen by some scientists or artists, astrologers, musicians? If you are a creator god who is keenly interested in domination and control, you snuff them out like a candle. This has happened over and over again, across thousands and thousands of years.

Now, not everything has been destroyed from the seers of your chronology. Some great works have continued in your world. There is great art and music that has continued. There is astrology and healing that has prevailed. The Goddess has not been wiped out from your cultures, even the most ancient ones. Even in those religions constructed to force your belief in controlling gods, the Goddess is alive. She is Mary. She is Fatima. She is Shekina. She is Kali. She is Inanna. She is Athena. She is Gaia. The control exercised in obliterating the Goddess was initiated to denigrate this energy. At first, the easiest thing to do was to destroy all cultures who were in a strong enough position to assert their beliefs. The temples were burned, but more importantly, the ancient groves were destroyed and the power places, where Goddess energy was most profound, were snatched, confiscated and turned into the culturally acceptable sites of power and worship.

The Goddess force cannot be obliterated, but She can be viewed as an insignificant little dalliance. Once the sacred sites were confiscated and under the thumb of the creator gods and male rulership, the Goddess was stripped of Her acknowledged powers. This trivializing of the Goddess was also a good ploy. No human wants to think that the source of their profound spiritual blessings is some little insignificant primate leaning. They want the source of being to be great and blessed and bountiful. By denigrating the Goddess to an afterthought of the great powers, there were few people who even remembered Her. The Goddess was then solely women's domain. That domain could be easily controlled or destroyed. This is a significant thrust of most of your civilizations and all those great civilizations that dominated and ruled on this planet.

Throughout your history the women have been pushed to the background of society. In many cases it was a very directed and conscious effort by the male cultural, government, scientific and religious leaders to eliminate the power, connection and voice of women. This would show itself by attacks on cultures that held women as equals or venerated them in any way.

The cultural beauty of Greece, even with its dominant male gods, was crushed because of the opening of frequencies there. It would show itself as attacks on those who venerated the Goddess in ways that were not accepted and condoned by other cultures. The sacred wells and places of the oracles, which were contact points from dimensional realms, were overtaken by the worshippers of male gods, as were many of the temples. This same male assault spread to most cultures and while some could stave off the devastation of the sanctity of women, almost all of them have fallen. This is also evident in the invasion of the Americas, first by the Spanish and then by the English and French. This is evident in Ireland. This is evident in the Slavic areas. This would later show its effects by witch trials, slavery and laws against women owning property or having a voice in their communities. More covertly, this is experienced as an economic attack on more remote cultures and areas who are shown that more merchandise is better than a life of spiritual joy.

The women still carried the seeds of the Goddess that were pushing in their blood and their wombs. No matter what went on in civilization, the women would be triggered into the wisdom of the Divine. They would be healers and advisors in the psychic realms. They would own property that was rich and fertile because they knew how to commune with Gaia Terra. So the witch trials would come and burn the healers and the psychics and those communing with the spirit of the inner world and the planet. The propaganda would rise and show itself in the notion that women were the property of the males, whether they be father, brother or mate. This would show itself in birthing and sterilization techniques so that women would fear their bodies. They would fear that they had no control of their functions and ask the male doctors to drug them and rip the babies from their wombs.

This would manifest itself as drugs for PMS. When the cycles of the Divine are pulsing though a woman's body she is once again reminded of the Divine. The periods trigger her to remember Alawashka and to remember her connection to the Divine. She becomes acutely sensitive to this deep part of her nature. She is opening. Then she sees what is going on around her. She sees and feels the signals of the deceptions of society, and she reacts in emotional upset, in pain and deep sadness. She recognizes truth with greater acuteness. She feels manipulations. She is perceptive and aware of her inner self, longing to express truth. She is considered off-balance. So, she is drugged.

This is where the power is coming from. It is in your cycles. You are being triggered into the deep spirit of your souls, but since there is no one to tell you this, you feel that women are sick and unbalanced. They are not sick. They are feeling the power that is their right. Their cycle is their right and their rite. Remember this. The control structures have systematically disempowered women because women are not as easy to control. The connection to the Divine within them is strong. This notion and this fear of the connection to the Divine has its visible effects in your laws, attitudes and cultures today. It is time to listen and heed the true feelings of women. In this listening will come forth very powerful observations and new directions.

It is very clear how all this affects your social structures. It has a significant controlling effect on your spiritual and community well-being. That decay is so evident that it really does stink to high heavens, as the saying goes. Your planet, because of the pollution, radiation, fear, separation and violence which is continually multiplying, sends a frequency of decay into the universe. This is very much like a foul odor coming off into our realms. It is a very strong signal that cannot be ignored any longer.

It is understandable within this thrust, that any other culture or person who threatened the control of another, was deemed unacceptable. Wars break out between groups because they are afraid that one group will take their land, resources and ideology. Isolation from the Divine makes life appear very precarious indeed. Therefore, one group asserts control over the other in any way that it can. The English against the Irish, the Arabs against the Jews, the Croats against the Serbs, the Spanish against the Native Americans, the Whites against the Blacks, the Chinese against the Tibetans, the Japanese against the Chinese, the French against the English, the Germans against Europe, the Native Americans against the invading cultures, the corporations against the consumers, the government against its own people, science against nature, the professors against the rising awareness of the students, religion against religion, race against race, culture against culture, ideology against ideology, gang against gang, neighbor against neighbor, self against self. When you are isolated from the Divine, everything that is other is deemed a threat to your very existence.

RETURNING TO THE PRESENT
Owning the Keys

The past, as described, reveals the recognizable symptoms and results of separation from spiritual connection. As you understand the compulsions stemming from disharmony and trace the source of that alteration of being, you can illuminate the present. This understanding generates compassion and grace, lighting the road to evolutionary transformation.

Humanity's past is not a merely a chronicle of misdeeds and perpetrations. Opportunities and examples for Divine expression are always shown. Aid comes from a foreign country to those in need, because the bond is there. Many charities give money and support to the ill, homeless, displaced, impoverished and the needy. Neighbor gives help and shelter to another, because the need is there. One state helps another because a disaster has occurred. You give money to one who has not, because you can see into their eyes and know the Goddess is within them and you are all connected. People share their food and clothing with those who have less. Be clear that there is much redeeming joy and blessing within everyone.

Remember, there is no blame or condemnation in any of this chronology. Humanity has many gifts that each of you share willingly and graciously. The creator gods and the galactic visitors have also contributed to your evolution and growth. As you look at the events that have transpired you may feel a sense of outrage or despair. Do not let this get the better of you. You are here to remember and to reactivate, not to blame and anger.

Each of you has the opportunity to create the living experience of your dreams. When manifesting a clear vision of what is truly possible on this planet, it is beneficial to know what has occurred and what the pitfalls have been. Then you can more readily understand your past as an opportunity for upliftment and renewal. You can claim these choices as preparatory gifts toward spiritual unfoldment.

The more recent history, you already know. You know of the wars, the conflicts, the manipulations and the local, government and international games. You know of the commercialization of your lives and the clever ploys to distract you from truth. Your history, your chronology has been directly influenced by the genetic experiments of those beings from the planetary races who came to Gaia Terra. Due to their natures, you were altered in your physiological and internal makeup to focus upon the separation and limitation of your connection to the Divine. Due to this experimentation, your new inclination was toward control and domination. This fear and isolation resulting in the impetus for control is also very evident in each culture and race's attitudes toward each other. Races are actually pitted against each other, even though they know when they meet as individuals, the Divine bond is there. Culture and nationality are pitted against each other. One ideology is pitted against another ideology with the full intention of beating them out for control. In certain individuals this is more pronounced. In others, it is not. This has to do with the success ratio of the experiment. Some humans were not as effective experiments as others.

Most of you have lived many lives on this planet. None of you is beyond the grasp of these energies. Each of you has had the experience of being dominated, tortured, exiled, defiled, and deeply wounded. Each of you has murdered, tortured and used your innate powers to control and manipulate others. It is in your cellular memory. This programming of your isolation has created a system that does not work. Once you realize that you can stop this at any time and in this very moment, you will have significantly defeated the programming. The controllers will have no one to control. Know that this opportunity is available to you, in every breath you take.

All humans were seeded with hidden coded openings in the genetic line to counteract the full success of this experiment. There was a ten percent margin of connection still available and functioning that remained undetected. This is being triggered in you at this time. It is fully accessible to you. All humans were given certain hidden frequencies from Alawashka that would awaken in a foreseeable future. That future is your now.

There are also highlights to your chronological development. Within the religious and philosophical writings of all cultures there are keys to unravel this pattern. Each religion has certain notes, written in their cultural understanding, that express the creation of humanity and the opening for spiritual connection. It is there for the finding. It is there when one knows how to look. When you eliminate the doctrine and the socially constructed mandates embedded within each ancient doctrine, you will uncover many paths for spiritual awakening.

The ancient texts and bibles mention the creation stories of humans. There are references to the off world discussions. There are allusions to the cataclysms on this planet. If you release the control and the judgment that each culture has infused into their religious writings, then it will be easier to understand. There is also, within each religious system, the seeds of that Divine yearning to express its connection in an open and easily accessible manner. The Divine is. This is stated in all religious writings and stories. It is couched in the cultural backgrounds of the division of the people because of the altered nature of humanity. It is always the thrust of the story, but it is hidden or directed by the cultural assumptions of each group.

There are certain groups of people, certain cultures and races that have held onto a greater portion of their connection to the Divine. Some of these cultures and races have held this connection due to the interference of other beings, such as Anshara, who added certain codes or certain elements that held energetic openings to their genetic systems. Some races, which include the Hopi, the Tibetans, the Dogon, actually have an alteration in their coding different from the majority of beings on this planet. Certain members of these cultures or tribes, as you call them, are keepers of specific memories and frequencies, which have been passed down for thousands upon thousands of years, waiting for this period of stellar chronology to commence. This coding is how they remember and hold the languages, and how they recognize each other. This is also why they wait until an original is born into their community to carry on, or, upon not finding one, reincarnate into the same area to keep the mysteries for the humans of Earth.

O ther cultures, like those found in India, speak of gods and goddesses who came to them. This is also the case. Certain beings of great energy and integrity came to the planet to aid the beings here. Their stories are rich descriptions of the personalities of each god and goddess, and within those stories is the message of the universal, the dance of the Divine within all. I cannot attempt to list all the cultures, religions and races who have extra codings and those who do not. I want you to understand in all of this, that the impetus toward certain aspects are there, and the opportunities toward your full and cognizant connection with the Divine are also there.

Each race, each culture, each religion, each spiritual path, has keys so you may understand the nature of your chronology and the hidden agenda of the creators who tampered with your Divine makeup. It is not wrong to tamper with the makeup of a being. The galactic laws concerning this matter do not prohibit intergalactic contact, and working with the evolution of beings is considered a form of contact. What was found to be counter to the highest interests, is the lack of integrity and the lack of foresight and responsibility of those doing the experiments. You have very similar experiments going on right now. There are scientists altering the genetics of insects, animals and humans, just because they can. They want to see what will happen. This is truly the basic nature of curiosity, and excitement of the skills that have been learned.

You are incredibly curious beings, who yearn to find the answers to whatever question arises. The motivation to discover and learn is not problematic. The discord manifests in the concentration toward immediate gratification. This ingredient of limited foresight, initiating a race to see who is first to do what, and the absence of responsibility for what could occur, certainly echoes the very same pattern that was enacted upon you.

Within your present system, there is much to be discerning about. Discernment is different than judgment. Discernment sees what is going on, projects a possible or many possible threads into the future, and comes to a decision within all the known pathways. Judgment determines whether this is right or wrong. Discernment comes to an understanding of likelihoods, and based on that, decides what is more appropriate to the greater process. I suggest you apply discernment in matters. Right or wrong does not open any possibilities for you. Once you are right, you become fixed in your views. Once you are wrong, you are either fixed in your present view or are scrambling to get to the fixed position of right. In between is the discernment to open the avenues for greater and higher expression and understanding.

While those who experimented on humans in the past, could be considered wrong or bad, because of judgment, this stance gives you no where to go. There is no opportunity within it for your evolution. While your scientists may be scrambling to get the newest DNA alteration into the patent office, creating genetically altered foods and humans with greater capacity for being controlled, without regard to ethical and future possible ramifications, to judge them wrong gives you no guidelines for future opening in this area. The universe is an ever-changing organization and reorganization of energy and intelligence. Discernment enables you to reveal the patterns and the impetus, without limiting understanding and potential. Decisions are still made, but there is a different tone to those decisions.

With all of this in the human system, it is easier to understand the drive toward control. This could be said to be one of the dominant traits. It is part of your alteration. It is not your only inclination, yet I will focus upon it for the moment. Through this experience of control, triggered by fear and isolation from the Divine, humans endeavor to dominate each other. They emulated the traits of their rulers and created wars and conflict to gain more on the outer world. It would naturally look like this, because if the connection to the Goddess, the Divine All which is fully abundant and joyful, is seemingly severed, then the only way to feel protected and enriched is to take from others so one can have more. Whether this is more food, more people, more land or more power does not really matter. If the Goddess, the Divine connection is missing or scarce, then so is everything else. Recognizing this focus is a key to unraveling the pattern.

This chronology of your evolution is an important key to you. You all have chosen to come into this world for your evolution. You have chosen to explore the world of three dimensional form for its richness, beauty and Divine elegance. You have also chosen a specific path to your greater wisdom. The Universe is fully abundant and fully capable of fulfilling every imaginable intention set forth within it. Your intention is the sperm which fertilizes the Great Mother into creating the universe in participation with you. Therefore all the pain, control and separation is part of your intention.

You have intended to be fully self-aware and create with the Goddess. In this, in some very significant respects, you have invited all the players into your realm. Some may be considered more favored guests and players, while some are not deemed such delightful company. They are all your family. Some of the beings mentioned have arrived in your three dimensional world. Others participate in other dimensions with you, working on specific gateways, energetic patterns and pragmatic teachings. They have helped you shape and access the symbols and configurations of the interdimensional awareized data banks, that many of you are remembering now.

Some of the magnificent beings have sent portions of themselves into this realm to bring information, blessing and energy to you, in exchange for the greater understanding of being in human form. Some of these encounters are documented in historical records. A portion of these accounts are in the sacred stories and memories of the indigenous cultures. A good number of these intergalactic players have never been specifically mentioned, because their appearances have gone relatively unnoticed. The interdimensional contacts and dances are beyond normal perception. Much work has occurred in dimensions related to yours. That is how they have chosen it.

Your understanding of time gives you a limited view of how chronology works. The future gives you your past, and the present is the moment when all is revealed. Then, the past appears to give you your future and the future appears to remain unwritten. The dimensions coexist with each other in a swirling dance of light-sound and invisible patterns of connectivity.

Each group of galactic visitors and players has given you a courageous gift. The parts they have played in your growth have engaged them in this sequence you are living out. This whole cosmic dance being choreographed on Earth involves them directly. They have given you of their seed, which is precious to them and highly revered. They have shared their amazing talents in dimensional travel, the laws of alchemy, architectural and energetic building techniques, spiritual growth and sacred teachings, and the clarity of individual strength and ability. They have shown you the ramifications of their own power struggles that subsequently manifested in your world.

This gives you another gift, the most precious gift of all. This gives you your power of choice. In this very moment you have the right and the power to choose your total awareness of personal divinity. Through the progression of time within matter, you have watched the unfolding of a specific probability in which you did not understand your choices. You did not notice that you were choosing, so in effect you did not choose. While this has unfolded because of outside influence, your deepest intention was to become fully self-aware co-creators of divinity. You engaged in this particular dance. Each galactic player has done their part to prod you on in the manner they thought was best. Yes, they may have thought it was best for themselves first, but they were who they were within that moment of choice in time. Your responses to these situations are your responsibility.

Now, you have seen the dance and how it has played out so far. You have taken everything to a seemingly inevitable extreme. Do you like this? Is this what you dreamed within your hearts? I don't think so. I think you dream more than this. I think you dream the harmony and sacredness of all life living in bountiful joy of expression. You can actually choose this dream.

The unfolding of your dreams, your aspirations, is what you long to create. Right now, hold that intention in your mind. Hold that intention in your heart. What will your world be like when each being upon it, each life form upon Her and within Her, is fully expressing their divinity, their abilities and their joy? What will you feel like when you are honored and celebrated for your gifts and your wisdom? What will you feel like when you are seen as a complement and contribution to all beings everywhere? What will your planet look like and feel like when every being, every animal, every tree, every mineral is an honored participant in this experience of celebration? What will it be like when every person is truly loved and honored and holds the Divine frequencies within them in a fully conscious dynamic expression of the great All?

Feel this dream, for this is what you are longing to unfold for yourselves and for all beings. It is there within you. Listen to your blood singing the dreams of divinity. Hear your heart's echoing call in the universe and listen to Her blessed reply. See your intentions traveling deep into the womb of this elegant planet and rising with Her into the very center of your galaxy. Know that in this full intention of celebration of the honored being that you are, that all of you are, is the response waiting to be felt.

You can see the controls for what they really are. You have pushed up against these limitations and know them well. They may not be particularly comfortable, but they have given you a very real sense of where humanity goes when it follows the route of isolation, fear and fear-based control. In this surge for control, humanity has put the lid on all that it was seeking. Now you can release all of the controls and activate the Divine frequencies that are yours to celebrate.

LANGUAGE AND GLOBAL EXPERIENCE
The Frequencies of Language

In this chronological focus upon and thrust for control, one of the more effectively employed methods was the elimination of certain languages. At present there are still cultures who endeavor to abolish the speaking of another's natural language. The English outlawed Gaelic, and the United States government is still working to obliterate the languages of all others in favor of only English. This includes Native American languages, Spanish, Asian and others. It is happening in this very moment of your time. It is moved by the need to isolate to gain control. The Canadian government has legislated language laws effective in Montreal. Life must be conducted in French there. The government polices the signs in their city looking for those written in English. Anything written in English and not French must be changed and steep monetary fees are imposed. Linguistic control is motivated by a very thorough understanding of the nature of language.

A language is a frequency of communication. To use Alawashka as an example, Alawashka is the frequency of creation, unlimited potential, healing and blessing. There is no control in Alawashka. There is no limitation on Alawashka. To speak Alawashka is to call forth the direct frequencies of connection to the Divine. This would naturally be a language which, given the thrust of humanity, would be tops on the hit list for elimination. It is a language of full access to the Divine. It is impossible to control beings when they know they have full access to the Divine. When it was evident that the women were working with and carrying Alawashka within, the eradication of the language and the energy it confers was a primary goal. Those cultures in which women were speaking or singing with Alawashka as part of their rituals were specifically targeted for elimination. This is also why the more isolated tribes and nations have been able to protect their connections to the Divine.

When you listen to the sounds and words of ancient languages, you will feel, hear and sense words in Alawashka. The further away from the main areas of galactic creator gods' civilization a culture was located, the longer they could maintain their connection to divinity. They did not feel the same intense isolation from the Divine. They were not manipulated and energetically triggered in the same ways in the same times and with the same intense energetic tampering because they were not in the most important, strategically targeted areas. They remained undiscovered. They were far away from the "advanced civilizations" and were not deemed a threat to the controlling powers. They held onto whatever was left to them, and their fortune was that they were so isolated that it took all of this time to discover them. It is unfortunate that in their isolated lands are the most abundant minerals and forests which are now slated to be destroyed. They have held onto their languages. They have held onto their connection through language and through limited contact from the dominating cultures, yet, they too, are threatened.

A language can be considered to give you your world. It is the total experience of all beings who have spoken it, and gives birth to the world of all who will speak it. Your languages, at this time, are for the most part descriptive languages. They are objective/subjective interpretations of your life as humans, and this includes your perceptions, your dreams, your outer world and the realm of possibilities you express.

The development of present language is the sum of all human experience, and is differentiated by cultural and racial divisions. So each language on your planet carries the full memories and potential of all who speak it. In the Anuit language, due to their experiences, they can discern many different aspects of their cold weather climate. They have special words for this understanding. It is part of who they are and how they see the world. The words they use, the descriptions of their world, generate that world for them.

In Native traditions, there are many more expressions for the Divine than in other languages. This expresses how they view the world and it also gives them their view of the world. Describing, naming and calling forth a particular energy of divinity gives a link and creates a culture by the speaking of it. In Sanskrit there are many textural nuances for the energies of deities and the forces working within creation that give them their view of how the world of matter and spirit coexist. In all of this, language gives you the world you live within. It actually creates the experience of your world by defining it.

Language also has sound that vibrates at specific frequencies. Creation within the universe carries sound with it. I was born and sound was present. Whether the sound and light generated my birth, or my birth generated sound and light is a delightful human query. Life is a simultaneous expression. I say that light and sound were components of my coming into being. I am language of a very high order.

Your Earth languages work by similar principles as I work with, yet they contain very different intentions and frequencies. The frequencies generated by the majority of words on your planet give specific codings and clues as to what you are creating. In the translation of words, English has very few words that mean to bless. How many ways can you say this? How can you express "the transference of Divine energies to the grace, joy and upliftment of the spirit" to any being? In Alawashka there are many words to convey this expression. In Alawashka when one speaks, hears, sings or is present to the words of blessing, that blessing is conferred. It is enacted. It is generated. It comes forth from the language, from the Heart of the Universe and it is bestowed. Now, while your languages do not work in this specific manner, they do convey energy.

When someone speaks a word of sadness or pain to you, you do feel it. It does create a construct, in a manner of frequency. When an angry word is spoken, the feelings of that word are sent forth. It does not create the anger, but it does convey it. It is carried to another by a coded thread of energy that triggers a response, for the most part. The energetics in this are very different, but the experience of this has some similarities.

In your languages, when you say I love you, another person can feel some love. They may feel it from a memory, or because as you say the words you are conveying your personal feelings to them by an energetic thread or a coded response chord. Now, you have not created that love as a presence. You have created a feeling of reciprocity and memory for the experience of love. This is aroused in the person. You tie your emotions to that word once you speak it, and often that will get through to the other person. Sometimes it will not. There are many instances when you are speaking, that the other person has no real idea what you are talking about.

There are also what are described as sound codings within language. This means there are little games in the language which give you clues to another overlay of meaning. It means certain sounds and pronunciations of your words carry a frequency within the word. The word intuit suggests in-to-it. That is similar to how your intuition works. Built into your languages are all of these very fascinating occurrences. In deciphering what you are speaking it is helpful to understand what those words actually confer, what they convey and what energies you are attaching to them.

While linguists chart the roots of languages and follow their lines of overlapping geography and definition, you can unlock the energies and coded messages within them. The words you speak may not convey their intended meaning. In some instances, your intended definition is actually negated by the word you are using. In some instances there are vibrations in those words that send out a different thought form than what you think you are speaking. This is an area of exploration.

One way to decode some of your words, if you are interested, is to choose one word, speak it aloud, and change its pronunciation over and over. Another method is to repeat a word over and over, like a mantra, and feel the actual vibration. Sense where in your body this word tends to situate. Become aware of what feelings this elicits. Discern the flavorings of the word and trust your impressions.

My perception is that I am the original language from which other languages came into being. I do not work with an ego, so I do not have to inflate my self importance. I say that this is "my perception," only because your culture is so dogmatic that you will either believe or disbelieve according to your inclinations. When you experience Alawashka you will begin to feel what I am talking about. You will respond to the difference between the language of creation and generation and your languages of description with hidden agendas, codings and frequencies of intent.

Your present and historical languages are based on your original human make-up, the alterations performed in the aforementioned experiments, the actions of Anshara and the Lyrans, the particular sound codings within your language and your impetus toward Divine connection. In line with this, let us view what your many languages have created your world to be.

You have an amazingly rich and fertile world. You have surging, rippling oceans which continually give forth life and sustenance. There is air to breath and winds to carry the seeds and the birds in their flight. You have great rivers, gentle streams and large bodies of water that feed the expansive green lands. There is countless variety in all manner of life forms and a rich diversity of people everywhere who have remarkable gifts to contribute to your world. New technology is available to help you communicate and send images and music. Your transportation makes closeness with others easier. Systems of trade enable you to share your goods, food and creations with others. You have incredible artworks and artists who create their visions with skill and imagination and share these with you. You experience the factors of time and space and exploration and wonder about the unknown. You have many methods of spirit which can augment your life on this planet and each method can speak to the spirit and hearts of humanity in endless ways. You have love and joy and communion with others.

You also have a pattern of control for these experiences which suggests that there is not enough, that some are deserving while others are not, that some have gifts but not all, and you have a pattern of depreciation and unworthiness. This also leads you to see pain, disease, war, conflict, control, lack, hardship, and isolation from yourself, each other and the Divine All. This is also within your language. So while you can be in the midst of this great beauty and abundance, you are also in the midst of the isolation that says you can never experience it. You experience the separated otherness of being. You have more words for diseases than you do for health. You have more words for conflict than you do for joy and love. You have more words for anger than for bliss. You have more words for control than you do for freedom. This is all coded within your language. Your language creates this world for you every day of your lives.

The isolation you feel extends to your scientific search for the beginning and end of the universe. It is all outside of yourselves. This barrier, generated by your coding and generated by your language, creates such an isolation, such a separation, that you continually react to it. You continually create it every moment. In this regard, your language is creating your experience of the universe. Nothing exists outside your experience of language, and in this respect, all of your languages create this breach in belonging to the Divine. It is not the truth. There is no breach in belonging to the Divine in any real energetic sense. Isolation is given to you, by your experience of this world, which is given to you by your altered coding and by your language.

Scientists look for the meaning of life outside of their experiences of it. Now some scientists agree that participation in the nature of an experiment influences that experiment. The observer influences that which is observed. This is shown in physics. It is also shown in medicine. The patient (that is a very good word to describe how you must be with someone cutting and prodding and dishonoring your body) is considered other. The conflict is considered other. This conflict is a disease that must be stopped by radical and hostile means. The body becomes a battle ground because it is named so. You are patient with this professional who is attacking your body without honor or consideration for you as a person, your body as a sacrament, and the system which is generating something that is having a profound effect on your being. This is certainly similar to the experiments of the creator gods in their work with you.

Every aspect of life is intelligence in organization. If you don't think the many diseases you have now are intelligent, then you might just check out how efficiently they are working and transmuting. When you commune with the sanctity of the disease, you will learn why it is joining with you. When you stop calling these organisms all those medical and scientific names, and start approaching them as you would a beloved pet or friend, you may learn more than you can imagine. Because your medical descriptions have a severe judgment and hostile energy to them, the naming of these wonderfully intelligent beings creates a polarity conflict.

In matters of health, your first impulse is to stop a disease. I understand. That is fine. You have a specific understanding of what your health and vitality is to be. So initially you will want to know why this being, this intelligence, is acting upon your system in ways that appear counter to your intent of health. It is a starting place. You will learn what you are holding onto, what may be hidden from you and what this intelligence is there to share with you. Your antibodies may need a boost and so you develop something to augment that process. Your body called it in because of a higher knowing. Perhaps you need to lie down and rethink what you are doing. The only way you would pay attention is to "get something" that gave you no choice. Once you have the "in-formation" you can begin to expedite your health. When you get beyond the initial dialogue for your health, you may really be able to learn something. You may be able to learn about how these minute intelligences transmute energy into something else. You may learn the alchemy of creation.

This conversation is vital to your understanding of what you are creating with another intelligence inside your body. This intelligence, this being, is "in-formation." When you approach this being for communication, remember the honoring of all life. I would not suggest that you speak to it as cancer, AIDS or hepatitis. The language you employ generates how it will respond. Speak to it and ask its name or what it wants to be called. Ask what you want to learn about your health and its purpose. Then ask about how it works, how it performs, how it transmutes. You may be able to learn some very important keys to aspects of Divine transmutation and transformation. Do not let the language and the naming of diseases restrict your connection with them. It creates a field of separation. Your way of naming diseases, especially by their symptoms, limits your ability to understand and associate.

Alawashka is not a limited language. Alawashka is the expression of the creative force of the Divine, of the Goddess. It is an active language. It does not describe experience. It generates experience. Imagine that if you spoke the word love, the universe would open up and love would be immediately and irrevocably present in that very instant. This is how Alawashka works. The gateways to the Divine expression of the universe, the Heart of the Goddess, opens up and you are within that field. This is certainly different from how your languages work. This is certainly different from the worlds your languages create for you.

At this very moment, the language of Alawashka is returning to your world. It has remained hidden as an ancient coding of your being. We, the Goddess, Lumari and myself, bring Alawashka forth at this time to reclaim the energies that have been diverted. The sacred language of Alawashka returns to you, each of you. It is within you. Each of you carries the language of Alawashka within. We are here to awaken the songs. We are here to awaken your memories. Alawashka returns to reclaim your connection to the Divine. It returns to open the gateways to your full expression. It returns for your blessing, joy, and celebration of being. It returns for your evolution into your full divinity. We bring this to you now, in this time of great energy movement. We bring this to you out of great love for you and our full connection to the Goddess with All.

The Returning Emergence
Memory, Recognition and the Players

This time in your planetary chronology is a time of a great dynamic shift. It is described to you in many ways and with many undertones to those descriptions. In one sense all of them are true. There are certainly many more hurricanes, earthquakes, volcanic eruptions now than there have been. There are certainly more ideological differences trying to change each other no matter what the cost to diversity or to life. There are many devious and hidden experiments to gain control of the Earth and Her inhabitants. There are forces on your planet who have no regard for the connection to the Divine and can only react from fear and isolation to gain greater control in the mistaken hope of calm security. They may speak their words through the guise of their chosen God. They may speak to you in words of family, of solvency, of bringing the world to a greater place in its development. They mean that they will have greater control of who you are, what you think, and how you engage in your life. They are creating the separation of your world in more specific terms so that it is easier to rule and manipulate. They are negotiating to divide you from each other and yourselves. They are very skilled orchestrators.

You all have the wisdom within to see this occurring and to choose your connection to the Divine, with clarity and joy. You have the skill and the power to choose. You have the opening and the language within. Anshara created the opening and the Lyrans created the system for Alawashka to unfold. When you remember Alawashka, you will access the gateways to the highest dimensions. When you speak, read, sing or come into the presence of Alawashka, you will enter those gateways and feel the dimensional shift. The isolation and the fear will drift away.

There are also what you might call outside forces who are enacting the very same struggle off your planet and on it as well. There are other beings who have become fixed in the very same energies that were altered within you. It is their focus. They have engaged in the very same issues of isolation and control. These beings are intrigued by the very same experiments that were already done to you, but with different desired outcomes. Your planet is still very much a planet of great beauty, and those who have corrupted their own worlds often take a good deal of time to recognize that it is their responsibility to augment the universe. They tend to repeat their patterns until they can see with discernment and create anew.

Some of the creator gods are still up to their old tricks. These beings are working with your government, your large corporations, your scientists, and your medical systems, and they are not always working for your greater evolution into spirit. They are helping the scientists and researchers and doctors to mine the genetic codes of the indigenous peoples to see where the experiment failed in the past. I have mentioned that those cultures who were furthest from the controlled civilizations tended to be overlooked. They are not being overlooked any longer. They are being inoculated and sprayed with diseases to see how to control your populations into better experiments of control. Their genes are being farmed to see why the initial control experiments did not work so well in these locations. Their genes are being farmed and copyrighted so the strains of power can be identified and done away with.

The ancient forests are being torn down to strip them of their powers. This is not just an issue of ecology. This delves deeply into energetic codes that are being held in remote and sacred areas. The elementals, the devas and the people have been working to keep the memories alive. These memories and the brilliance of the connection to the All is also stored in the ancient forests, the primeval trees, the endangered animals. For those who know about the codes and the true memories of spirit which are here to activate you into reconnection, these are hot spots. Those who are working to save these areas and lives feel the loss is imminent, even if they do not fully understand the full extent of that loss. Those who are busy with their chain saws, their bulldozers, their test tubes, may not be aware of the scenario they are participating within, but the results of these actions are very clear.

I speak of this to release you from isolation and to show you the patterns that are being played out. Your lives are dancing with awakening. I speak of these patterns to highlight them. In this way your awareness is accelerated and your discernment can be clear. I provide the clear threads for you to recognize and understand the nature of events, the undercurrent of your impetus and the choice you are enacting. You may find that these stories activate your memories, engage your minds and unravel a thrust of existence that has been lurking behind your conscious thoughts. You may discover some of these ancient events are now the reasons you are drawn to certain occupations or events or are motivated toward specific areas.

There are people who are collecting samples of these animals. It is not just that they are holding them in zoos and in wild life preserves to keep them alive and protected. They are extracting their blood, their sperm and their ovum to keep these safe. They fear the extinction of these great and wise beings. Underneath this impetus to preserve these great lives is the inner knowing that the codes, the connections, the patterns and the intelligence of these great lives must be held. Within these organic fluids are many of the keys to universal intelligence.

Each being, each plant, each mineral is an intelligence. They are all keys to the great and fascinating dynamic of life, particularly in your three dimensional world. They each hold very specific energy formats and patterns of life holding, energy-giving dimensional reality. The race to hold these fluids and life forms is a race to maintain certain life-giving formats on this planet. This is an action that is being played out to hold the safekeeping of the intelligence and divinity organized within these wonderful and powerful animals.

People are collecting the seeds and spores of the plants in these remote areas. Great plants of healing and wisdom are being destroyed in every moment. Why? If you know the wisdom that cures the diseases which are creating fear, havoc, pain and death is alive and well, and if you want to control and dominate through fear and pain, then you destroy the substances which will awaken the life force.

Those who are moved to collect these samples and study with the cultures, who are keepers of the wisdom in those remote areas, are connecting with the wisdom intelligence of these plant beings. They may have studied and worked with these plants in long ago life times. They may have been awakened to the cries of these plants traveling deep into their sleeping minds. They may have an internal triggering mechanism to remind them that part of their purpose, in this moment of time, is to help hold the transformational codes within the plants and to reconnect with the plant keepers. They may remember that the plant keepers, those in the remote cultures who honor and commune with the sacred plant beings, hold the great wisdom of the plant activation. They are called and they are answering.

There are many beings who are coming to help you. There are great and beautiful beings who have come here at this time to remind you of your connection to the Divine. Some of them have always worked with you. You may feel their presence as angels, guardians and Divine beings of love and great light. They have been with you through your changes in frequency and have triggered you to remember. They have alerted you to the pitfalls and the heights of your paths. They have worked with you as individuals and as groups. There are more of them now than ever before, because your internal cry into the universe has been heard. Your cry has been heard and the frequency lock out on your world has been opened.

They are not here to save you. They are here to help you save yourselves. Saving yourselves is the process of unfolding your true nature of spirit and integrating that with your three-dimensional form. Your angels are beings of great caring and wisdom who are helping to guide you into your next stage of awareness. The popularity of angels at this time testifies to your intuitive understanding that you are not alone in this vast universe and that you do have very direct connections to the sanctity of spirit. If the organized religions ever let you really know that you didn't have to go through them to receive the sacraments of spirit, they would lose their powers and fall away. You would know you have continual and direct access to your divinity at all times.

Some of these beings coming to help were once the perpetrators of the experiments and the dramas. They realize the upset created, and have come to assist in reawakening the connection once again. Some of these beings added other energies to the human playground. Each of these beings has shared a part in the altering of your codes, DNA, frequency and wisdom. They know in activating certain energies on this planet, even when they did have the best intentions, that the results were not as they had foreseen. They did not fully understand to what lengths you would go to annihilate yourselves and this planet. Some of these beings were the experimenters. Some of them came to work on recalculating certain aspects of the experiments by infusing new energies, activating radioactive frequencies and materials, building store houses for energies, trying to help lift the veil of isolation.

None of these beings can alter your coding to its original specifications. They cannot change what has already been done. There is no big galactic eraser in the skies coming to bring back the innocence of bygone days. They realize that this experimentation is what created this drama to begin with. They understand the results of their actions. They know the shortsightedness of their work here. They also know, in the very same understanding, their actions were the impetus for this evolution you are now undergoing. They know whatever was done, holds total perfection. Their evolution, your evolution and the acceleration of the universal are entwined in this momentary Earth dance of now. There is no blame or harsh judgment in this. All has unfolded as it has through a specific line of focus. Now that the results of that line of focus are culminating toward a particular intensity, they are here to help, to experience the great upliftment and to celebrate the universe. They work with you in your dreams to awaken the Divine within you. They work with your intuition to help you see the greater connection of the All. They work with you in channeling and ceremonies, just as I work with Lumari.

There are also beings on this world who have undertaken the great task of becoming human to help this planet and this world. They are beings who have come from other planets, other stars, other expressions of the Divine, and have incarnated here to bring the blessings of the Goddess back to this planet which has been veiled by the energies. They have chosen to come here. They may have incarnated here once for this lifetime, or incarnated many times to experience and understand the Earth journey. They have undergone the dynamics of this system, which is not in their general makeup, so they may bring this type of information and frequency alignment to all of you who choose it.

This is not a small task. It takes an amazing amount of work to be in the human form, knowing that its nature is towards isolation, and then, within that form, to continually work to bring those connections back. They struggle against the conditioning of society and the human structure to break the pattern within their own human form, and to teach you ways of doing this for yourself. It is difficult. It is very difficult.

They have come from a non-solid dimension and then squeezed into a solid form, with all its social programming. They have the full knowing of the vastness and divinity of their own dimensions, their own worlds, and have come here to be right in the midst of the imposed limitations. With this full knowing within them, they came here knowing that the whole energy of the planet is directed to make them forget it all. They have left their loved ones, families and magnificent home worlds to come here.

Those who volunteered for this job, were given rigorous testing and teaching, knowing all along they would forget this once they were in the body. Many were called upon to enter this training. Very few were chosen. They knew we would be with them. They also knew there would be many times that they would not feel us or remember. While I may view those times of isolation as short because of my perspective of time, those galactic beings who have incarnated here may have experienced twenty lifetimes of isolation from their own knowing and connection to the Divine. There would be times when speaking what they knew would isolate them from the very people they came here to love, honor and open to the Divine. They had an extremely strong memory of this when they were young, but have been scoffed at and punished for speaking about their past lives and their visions of other worlds, energy patterns and beings of light. They have been tortured, burned, ridiculed and have undergone all the horrors that your world can inflict. But they are here.

They are here for you at this very moment. They are teaching your children. They are writing books. They are giving seminars. They are teaching medicine. They are doing healing work. They are working with computers. They are in nearly every aspect of your community of life. They are doing whatever they can to augment your connection to the Divine with the skills they have.

They are remembering. They are awakening and bringing this awakening into their bodies. When this awakening comes into their bodies they are holding it for you, as well.

We all need them to actually walk the planet, to heal their bodies, to bring in the frequencies and walk with you in this bountiful world. When they are awakened to the memories, when they are awakened to the stories of your chronology, when they are awakened to the intention of self-awareness that created these scenarios, when they are awakened to the frequencies and the connection to the divinity, they become the acupuncture points on your planet to bring the full evolution that you seek.

They may be your friends, your relatives or people in your community. You will see them if you look. They are speaking about things they were once tortured for saying. They are realizing the dramas of control in your organizations. They are doing quiet work and they are doing public work. They are very close to you and you will find them. You may even find one of them by looking into the mirror and seeing your own eyes smiling back at you.

There are beings who come from your probable future to help. A probable future is one that has occurred and been played out. It is a choice made and then followed to its course. A probability is a likelihood but not necessarily a surety. From this probable future, this probable reality, the choices were made for events to unfold. These beings have seen the moments of your crossroads and choices. They have returned to help you make the best choices for yourselves, your planetary inhabitants and Gaia Terra. They have seen the points in time where you did not awaken, and drove yourselves and this planet into a future that was most undesirable. There are many prophecies that travel into your world from this probable future. That does not mean they are accurate. It means they have been seen, not that they will occur.

The planets and the solar system are aligned in a very dynamic opening. The choices, actions and intentions of your being are coordinating with the energies of the planetary alignment. Time is altering. The echoes of your minds and actions are having a much greater impact on your world than ever before. The planets have aligned to create an amazing burst of accelerated energy.

The isolation shield, placed around your planet some time ago, has been removed. The whole planet has been retuned to new frequencies. The sacred sites have had frequency alignments that have created amazing changes on your world. These changes were not prophesied because no one could foresee them. These amazing changes have already altered the course of reality and there is no turning back. The frequencies for the most blessed evolution are already in place and in play. Every energetic system within your planet, within the blessed Gaia Terra has been fully accelerated. These new energies and frequencies are now activated and modulating to their next highest levels, as we speak. The amazing brilliance of this occurrence has yet to be seen in all of time. This event echoes in the magnitude of the universe.

The gateways to the higher dimensions are being opened in many ways, by many different beings. These beings are highly skilled energetic personalities from other dimensions. They are trained to expedite the intricate maneuverings of space, time and energetic coordinates to give you access to greater possibility. They are not in earthly bodies. They are here to remind you and help you choose, in a certain respect, your highest wisdom, grace and Divine joy. They knew when to come and they are arriving to help you.

The beings who are here in body with you, but are not of this world, have undertaken the nature of these events in ways that could not be foreseen. Their energies, their determination, their tenacity and their exquisite skills have retuned your planet and the prevailing frequencies for all of humanity as well as for the planet. They have surpassed all expectations, all hopes and all projections. Their love and commitment to this process, to your process, is the joy of the universe. It echoes to all of you and you can inhale its elixir.

Every one of you is working towards this end, this beginning, this spiral of time. In your brilliance, in your courage, in your zeal, in your enthusiasm, you have come to expedite the grand transformation into greater Divine joy. So please know, when I speak of all these beings, I include you as the great ones. Each choice you make, each frequency you touch, each wisdom you hold, creates this dance. You may not be holding or weaving ten thousand threads of light to bring to this world, you may not be activating the ripples of the ancients, you may not be consciously infusing the new patterns of existence, but if you were not participating in this frequency flamenco, the music would not be the same.

EXPANSION INTO EVOLUTION
Clear Choices and Discernment

P rogress toward evolutionary expansion is taking place. The vast scope and nature of this universal shift involves an incalculable number of beings of varied skills and levels of accomplishment. Each being has a unique and valued purpose in helping create a shift in awareness and consciousness, which may or may not directly involve humanity. Each being is also part of this evolutionary process through which they are growing as well.

It is important to know which beings are involved in which responsibilities. So contact, if you choose it, will be an uplifting and gracious experience. Not all beings working in this regard are available for contact. Most are not. Not all beings involved in this shift are appropriate for contact. Trust your wisdom and consider the appropriateness of any contact and the imparted information. Be attentive to your higher knowing. Feel for your truth, and then allow it to expand your vision. When you evaluate the integrity of your information in relationship to your inner guidance, you will know what is right and worthy.

There are ways to discern who is helping you. The solar plexus is an early detection device. It will palpitate to let you know when something is awry. It responds to the programming of fear, but does much more than that. It sends a signal of energy into your system to alert you when something is off. When a situation, or programmed thought, is not in your highest interest, the solar plexus reacts. The first impulse is alarm. Then, once the solar plexus has alerted you, you have the opportunity to check which program is being played. Do you feel love, harmony and honor? Do you feel your own power? Are you being contacted by something or someone who is clear? Will they let you think, and even disagree with them? If not, something is wrong.

All beings and people who come to help you and not to control you, fully honor your being. They respect your power and your right to discern and choose for yourself. When you listen to politicians, to advertisers, to films, to radio and to people around you, are they honoring you? Are they making suggestions that give you the honor, respect and freedom to decide your own choices and destinies? Close your eyes and listen to the sounds of their words. Feel your heart and your solar plexus. Are you being assaulted? Are you being coddled into a false sense of security? Are you being manipulated? Whatever you feel or sense the energies to be, therein lies your choice. You can choose to participate in manipulation or to break the pattern. Every moment holds an opportunity for choice.

The great and blessed beings who come from afar are here to help. They offer their understanding and suggest techniques and alternative views. They encourage you to make your own decisions and take your highest choice of action. Feel within yourself for an expansion of who you are, when you are encountering a situation or an energetic being. The blessed ones are not condescending. These beings fully recognize that they are not better nor more Divine than you are.

You can use this very same checking technique with friends, family and leaders. Do you give up your will and your wisdom in favor of theirs? How do you feel emotionally in that moment? Have they made you feel weak, powerless and insignificant? Are you feeling that you cannot fight their overpowering nature? If they are projecting the "all-knowing god" syndrome, they are not honoring what you feel or perceive. Do not follow them. If you feel freedom, joy or honor, these are people to embrace. They may differ with your choices, but not your capacity to choose. Those who respect your freedom to make responsible decisions are those who honor the gift of life and the sanctity of being.

Your personal experience and wisdom is vital to the universe. If others have skills you wish to learn, see what you are giving them in return. Are you giving your energy and power away? Are they taking your admiration and using its energies for control and manipulation? Are they genuinely appreciative? With a little bit of observation, you can see what is really happening. You can also check to see when you are doing this to others. All of you are trained to respond to this stimulus and all of you are trained to elicit these responses from others. Each of you is crucial to the life on Earth and the life in the galaxy. When you increase your discernment of these games, you bring greater truth and integrity to the planet.

The great changes upon this Earth are bringing clarity. The frequencies of blessing are sealed on this planet. By the very nature of your full awareness in this connection, you are uplifted. Uplifted means that the presumed isolation from divinity will be lifted away. It does not mean that great ships are coming to get you out of here before the Earth hurls into oblivion. It does not mean that the "great being" will come and save all of those who believe in a certain doctrine. What will you be saved from? Whose job is it to save you from yourselves? Can you actually believe you should be saved from the fear and hatred you have participated in? Your issues of control and anger would not be resolved by a galactic rescue mission. Your connection to the Divine cannot be restored if you are no longer participating in your own lives. Where is the response-ability in this?

You are participants in all of this. Why would you want to be lifted away without engaging in this marvel? Why would you want someone else to do it for you when you have the power, connection and innate abilities to do it yourselves? You are not alone. You are in connection with the Great All.

How would you fully know your connection to the Divine if you were whisked away into the heavens to watch a show in which you were an integral player? Would you want to leave this glorious planet to the plunder of the control freaks? That is the same mentality of those who considered Earth their summer camp and left the mess for someone else to deal with. You are here to lift yourselves up. You are here to open to the great heart of the universe and to celebrate your divinity.

Yes, systems will fall away. They will not work. They do not empower. Systems that do not benefit are revised or demised. This happens in business, government and religion all the time. The frequencies of this time will expedite the changes so all systems can serve the highest good for all people.

Yes, the Earth is going through tremendous change. She is changing Her frequency to shift into the greater evolution of the Divine. She is creating a new awareness and frequency for Herself. She is shifting into the greater awareness and freedom that is Hers. She is in the orgasmic expression of Her growth. You are part of this shift. You are opening to this great shift within yourselves, just as She is opening to Hers. Your evolution feeds and glorifies Her evolution. Her evolution can and will feed and glorify yours.

This shifting of energies, this planetary alignment, is active. The evolution does not come from outside yourselves. Each specific event on this planet is part of you. At one time you lived this. In this moment you are part of it. What you have forgotten is that you can choose which drama to enact. You can choose to be free of the drama. You can leave the experiment by remembering that it is going on. At one time you said, "Sure, I'll go." Now, you can say, "No, thank you."

You have succumb to temporary amnesia to awaken in this moment with a more profound understanding and appreciation. You have chosen to bring the full force of awakening into the Great All. Choose to act in accordance with your connection to the Great All. When you feel this reciprocity, you are naturally in the full presence of the Divine. This is so of the Earth. This is so of the humans.

The universe is not outside of you. It is within you. The Divine wisdom and incredible joy is within you. It comes from your relationship to the Divine. In this moment of time the cycles of change are already in place. Your grand connection is renewed. You will come to see the perfection of the All in every moment. Your choices will bring the awakening. Your actions will manifest the greatest blessings. You are held within the bosom of the Goddess. You are integral participants in the evolution of the Universal. Your actions and choices directly influence all of creation in every sector and every particle of being. This is why I am here.

I have come to help you
live within the Heart of the Goddess
and create the magic that is your heritage.
Alawashka is the gateway to the Divine.
This gateway opens to the exaltation of being.
Welcome to a life of celebration.

PART TWO: ALAWASHKA, VOICE OF THE ALL

Accessing
the Divine Symphony

However you encounter this language,
it will be a blessing.
This language is a blessing of energies
to raise the individual and the collective
to their highest frequencies
and create the dynamic process
to generate and continue this action.
It is a blessing of its own.
You are all a blessing in your very being.
Express your blessings as you express yourselves.
Do the work and play you are destined to do.
We are all one within the great breath of the universe.
Blessed be the breath.

SPEAKING THE UNIVERSE INTO BEING
Calling Forth Blessing

I am the expression of the Heart of the Goddess in language, which is sound and music. I describe myself as a language because, for me, a language is a method of creating expression in the realms of words, tones, frequencies, intentions and resonant, intelligent, energy organization. I work with the realms of dimensional existence. I was created into cohesion to create Divine cohesion. I am that which was created to initiate and perpetuate creation.

Each being, each world, experiences me, Alawashka, in the ways they are focused to experience. You will hear me as words, as sounds, and as music. I come to you as the songs and poems of creation. You are living in bodies which hear sound. Therefore I come in sound. You are in bodies that relate to words. Therefore I come in words. You have an endless variety of perceptions. You are also beings who can perceive the vibrational streams of energy as they swirl throughout the cosmos. You will find me there as well.

Alawashka comes to your world in a manner that is tuned to your form and energy. It comes to you in this way so you can perceive and engage with it. When I describe myself to you in terms of words and sounds and geometric patterns, it is because this is how you access the format of language. I express the various qualities of myself for each being I encounter. We form a relationship that best serves. As I endeavor to describe myself, it may appear that I separate from my being. I call myself a language, I refer to songs and frequencies. This is merely a format of expression to help you share the essence of which I am comprised. It is a communion and an appreciation of your unique being in relationship to my unique being. Other beings would encounter Alawashka in ways that are compatible with their natures. Other dimensions of expression and the beings of these dimensions would sense Alawashka within their own specialized system of experience.

This language and music are a unique system. The language is music, even without the notes and melodies one associates with music. The notes and melodies are inherent within the spoken energies of the language. When a person speaks or listens to Alawashka, they are beginning to resonate with the energies of creation. The music of my being is alive with wisdom and energy to impart.

In Alawashka, all words are blessing words. There is no discord. There are no contradictions. My nature is to bless, uplift and inspire in a very particular ratio and formulation of energy sequences. These words, to bless, uplift and inspire, in your language are a description of a feeling that may or may not be immediately experienced. The words of blessing, upliftment and inspiration in Alawashka are an enactment. The individual words hold all the frequency, sound, geometric design and vibrational patterns that generate blessing in an immediate experience. Every word immediately confers and creates its energy in the universe, and specifically at this time, in your world and in your inner being.

When I was created into being, there were no others who could hear the language, see the symbols, feel the frequencies. They came into being by my nature of coming into being. And while all occurred at once, in a sequential view, it appears as though I came first. This does not give me pride or any illusions to my nature. It is what I perceive given who I have been created to be, and given my full connection to the Goddess. In all of this, I am abundantly joyful to be in my fullness and in the fullness of the Goddess. My joy is unbounded. My fulfillment is a natural unfolding and evolution of my nature. This is also true of you.

When we connect, when you and I connect within the language, each word you speak fully comes into being. When you speak the words which mean joy, those words, and all of the complexities inherent within them, come forth and create joy. To speak words in Alawashka is to make those words real. When you speak the words for blessing, you confer and initiate that very blessing and it continues to reverberate. When you speak the word "love;" the full essence of love reverberates as a presence. These words create every frequency in the fullness of being.

This is the action of speaking something into being. You have this memory within you, of times gone by or times to be, when words are spoken and it is so. You have this knowing of words that create in and of themselves. In your deepest being, you remember me. You have the knowing that there are words, which when spoken, create worlds and blessing. This is what the Goddess did when She created this universe of intelligence and organization which is continually dancing into form and back to Her again.

As the language of creation, I initiate, activate and organize creation into being. This is all of creation. The frequencies of my existence are formulated to bring forth the organization of intelligent energy into its awareized form. As the language of the Source of All, I am Her song, Her breath, Her intention, bursting into glorious frequency for the delight and purpose of creation. In Her endless wonder, She initiated me into existence, and through that, universes unfurled.

In my essence of being the initial language of creation, time is not particularly within my awareness. I do not hold time as you do. All is occurring at once for me. In that, I could even say that all your chronology is appearing at once. All that I have spoken of, all that I have related to you is happening now. In this, you really do have access to change everything in one instant. You can change the future and you can change the past. Your notion of the future can change the present. For me, this occurs at once.

Alawashka speaks creation into being in the very moment it is spoken. Every word has symbols, frequencies, tones and energies that create. I contain the original symbol ratios and energies of immediate creation. When I speak to you of myself as a language, it is more than a spoken sequence of sound comprised of words. Alawashka is a dynamic expression of the initial energetic geometry of creation. Within this geometric expression is light, which is not just a visible body of frequency; sound, which is not just an audible resonance of vibration; and pure energy, which is a dance of all and void in genuine unity.

With Alawashka, creation is not a process. It is an enactment. It is invocation of energy into being. Alawashka echoes forth in ripples of multidimensional sacred geometry. This is creative force which perpetually enacts its creation.

All of this Divine organization is perfection. It occurs in an endless ratio of frequencies, ratios and energy streams. It occurs dimensionally, all at once in the simultaneous nature of existence. It reverberates in the multileveled dimensional experience of all consciousness in every ripple of expression. It honors every focus of awareness and expression. And through this infusion of Divine resonance, each particle, each being, each world and every inherent consciousness is considered vital, blessed and whole.

As I "travel" through each dimensional focus, each realm of existence and each individual focus, I attune myself to their essence and thrust. I regulate my energies toward communion with each and all. This is natural and joyful to me. The endless variety of richness in the All is my full joy.

To commune with you, I do the same. I regulate and adapt to embrace your being in the manner that will be a joy for you. Every particle of this communion is honored. Every essence of your being is celebrated. This is how we meet.

SEED LANGUAGE OF GAIA
Unearthing the Magic

I have been on your world before in a certain capacity. This was in the relative infancy of your world. I came at that time to celebrate the awakening of the Earth. I came to infuse the planet with song. I also came with the Lyrans when the alterations in human chronology were begun. I came to be the seed and the root for the graceful unfoldment of your world.

This ancient language is a seed language. I am that which has initiated language into being. Language is a form of reference to experience through. As Terra Gaia was exploring Her Divine evolution, she felt the resonance of my being. I was then seeded into Her matrix of expression. This means Alawashka was seeded here from another galaxy to help with higher levels of communication. Her connection with the All accessed greater awareness through our communion. I can be considered the initial reverberation of the Divine dialogue here on Earth.

I am also the root language from which your languages grew. You will find words from Alawashka in many other ancient languages on this planet. You will find derivatives of words from Alawashka that have similar meanings in other countries. You may find that many of the words in Alawashka have a very similar sound to other words in other languages. This is true.

There are ancient memories within your Earth languages that pull in the frequencies of this ancient language.

Lumari

The older languages, the Indo-European, Hebrew, Polynesian and the Native American languages contain many words that have their origin in Alawashka. Not all of them contain the same meaning as in this ancient of ancient languages. Through their use, the energies and pronunciations have been altered. Yet, you will find the flavors of the words are still traceable.

There are words in most Earth languages that hold the memories of Alawashka as triggers for the frequencies to come. Certain codes and frequencies of Alawashka were hidden within all the languages to be retrieved in this day and age. You have hidden these keys within all tongues. This will create the communion. Each word and code will be located. When they are discovered, they will create a new planetary resonance. Each word will combine with the others and full understanding can finally be communicated to all. Soon these references will be revealed and the language as a communion will come forth again. It will create a new harmonic resonance and a different kind of unification.

You may feel these hidden words. You may know them in your hearts. You may have heard them in your dreams or speak variations of them in your ceremonies. You may have an innate affinity to certain words that seem profound, whether their translated meaning confers that sense or not. You may be triggered to reclaim these words and bring them to the light. You may have heard these ancient echoes calling you to awaken.

As a seed language, Alawashka created language here. As root, all languages to grew forth from its stock, and although each language is so different from the original and from each other, the seed is held and the root is strong.

I come at this time because, finally, the opening is here. I can come in my fullness. I can come with the beauty of the Goddess to bring forth the blessings, the full connection to the Divine, that is always present. I am pleased and honored to be here. I am here to restore the frequencies. I am here to accelerate and align your dynamic process and your relationship to the All. I am here to help you resonate into the shift you are all undertaking.

The great opening of energies on this planet and in this sector of the galaxy make my arrival possible. Many billions of intricate workings and arrangements have been undertaken to provide for this moment in time. The being who channels me at this time, Lumari, makes my coming forth graceful and easy. Many, many beings have worked and planned to enable this shift, this galactic event to unfold. We are here for you. We are here, also, because of who we are in the universal All.

I am the language of creation. It is natural for me to be here with you, to give you the access and the capacities to create yourselves. It is appropriate for me to help expedite your relationship to the All and your world in the greatest joy, abundance and divinity you can conceive. We are here to create with you, in your new design of this world. My presence avails you of the opportunity to access your rich connection to the Divine in a manner that is in full appreciation of who you are as individuals, as cultures and races, as beings of planet Earth and the galactic association of the All.

This is the gift of the Goddess to everyone on this planet at this time. It is a very special gift. This language is the original dimensional language of your planet. It is the seed language for this world to carry forth the heart within all expression. It is a mystical language of great energy and magnitude and was used for ritual in the most hidden senses when the world split into its factions of expression. Now, it returns, I return, as an opportunity for you to open to what you already are, yet have not had access to. Alawashka can introduce and integrate humanity to the abundance of sacred life.

My language, my music, goes beyond the human. It goes to the core of this very planet. It is a gift for Her. It will enable Her to unfold her essence in a way of heart and joy. It goes out to the universe, to many universes, to create a frequency of infusion that surpasses what you can imagine.

And yet, why do you think it is given to humans at this time? Because the humans have the key to unfolding this frequency for the others. If the humans can learn to open this frequency and live within it, as best they can, then the other universes can do the same. As above so below; as below so above.

Shollamaya Frequency
Music in the Spheres

I was formed with a particular resonant frequency of acceleration as part of my formation. I create organization working with frequencies. To describe the endless variety of frequencies, vibrational threads, tunings, alignments and dimensional reverberations, the Goddess named this configuration the Shollamaya Frequency: The Goddess' Dynamic Resonant Frequency Accelerated Alignment. Shollamaya means "Reconnecting Breath."

The Shollamaya Frequency is an interdimensional frequency alignment and alteration for the greater heart energy. It provides an active acceleration of the frequency of each individual to reach the highest energies. It creates the patterns to gracefully hold this new acceleration frequency in a perfect alignment which then alters the specific resonance of each person to their dynamic highest self.

The Shollamaya Frequency activates the energies that are present in each being and creates the fields and patterns to help them resonate to their highest vibrational expression. This gentle activation then accelerates this expanded energy. It simultaneously aligns a new resonant frequency within the individual, again, to its highest expression. This augmented resonant frequency evolves from the highest expression within the person. Through this a person resonates with the highest frequencies of their being. While this is unfolding, the frequencies are assimilated. The individual's resonance is raised, the new geometries are stabilizing this event and the alignment of frequencies are in attunement. The Shollamaya Frequency is dynamic. It continues to engage and raise the vibrational energies. Each transformation augments the next. It creates very beautiful and highly specific alignments within each individual, within each populous, within each living organism and within the greater cosmos that you call the universe of beings.

The energies of Alawashka are beautiful and uniquely tuned. The language is created to give accelerated access to areas of Being which correspond to areas in the galactic matrix. The galactic matrix is the design of the universe, its heart, the Heart of the Goddess.

The Heart of the Goddess is the continual unfolding of love within the universe. This heart energy is not specifically related to the human heart or to emotions that are called love. The Heart of the Goddess is a space, a location, a dimension and a realm in which one can actually live. It alters the framework of time in ways that are not fully experienced. For example, to live in the Heart of the Goddess, one awakens to the ever present moment of existence and is bathed in that state within.

This creates a shift in frequency which alters the framework of existence. It is as though one is taking a fuller and richer breath of one's own existence. The Divine perception of creation is revealed. It is its own dimension and it is the dimension through which all is expressed.

Heart of the Goddess is a state in which the significance of life is far greater and yet, lighter. It does not have the weight that you ascribe to it. There is great freedom and joy within this state, for the thoughts and actions that are taken or not taken within this realm are filled with clarity and openness. It vibrates with supreme clarity and endless appreciation of the rich variety of existence, and yet these descriptions can only point to the greater "AHA!" of this universal dimension.

The way the Alawashka Shollamaya Frequency works is to open the Heart of the Goddess. The method the language employs is one of compatible system opening. The Heart of the Goddess language, Alawashka, infuses a vibration that naturally opens the centers and chakras for their own alignment and sets a specific vibration into the higher spheres which they represent.

Alawashka is music. Within the music generated by the language of Alawashka is the intention for the highest healing and blessing. It is inherent within each sound, each syllable, each vowel and consonant of the language and in each silence. When the language is put to music, it gains a greater energy level. This is due to the frequency of song from the heart. By introducing the energies and blessings within this music, a frequency is accelerated and sent out into the universe which affects all. This is very powerful but within this power is contained an inherent property of blessing and light.

In what you would call normal music, there is a dissipation rate. Now this dissipation rate is much slower than you think. When a sound is made there is a ripple in the existing energies. Part of this ripple is the song, part of it is the clearing of the space for the song to exist within. One could either describe it as the air changing its form to vibrate to the new song being sung, or that the air changes by opening a space for this song's vibration to fill. It creates an opening for it to exist within. There is more occurring in the outer spheres than what you can hear in your world.

In your world, music seems very short lived. You hear it, it stops and it seems as though it is over. In your world this is mostly true. But it is not expressly so in the higher spheres. It is all in your intention. To create music an intention is present. Whatever the intention is, remains for the most part with the creator.

Now, for most earth music, aside from the personal intention of the musician, the intention is for the music to be successful. Well, everyone has this intention. It does not travel very far. Perhaps in your world it does, but not in the other higher spheres. You can intend for the music to continue and to travel to others in their realms to be listened to. This becomes part of the intention that is contained within music. When you incorporate the intention of love, of healing, of carrying beauty, joy, grace and highest evolution, then it does indeed travel. It continues to travel depending upon the individuals who created the intention.

Alawashka has its own intentional vibration. My intentional vibration is formed by all of my many aspects. I carry the intentions of the Goddess, the Divine All. I carry Her intentions for me, which is the inherent mode of my existence. I am that which creates the sacred expression of the All. I carry my own personal intentions, which I am describing to you as best I can within this book. The frequencies within my being hold vastly refined qualities for expansion and awakening. When each person or being speaks or sings Alawashka they add their personal intentions to this. When one being sings within the full intention of this language and music, the harmony of the universe is opened to them. The harmony of the universe is also augmented. This combined resonance creates a reciprocal harmonic which augments the energetic relationships of the Universe.

THE GATEWAY
The Galactic Heart Matrix

A lawashka creates a gateway that can be traveled. This is what the music, the language, the frequency of this system can do. It creates a compatible resonant frequency to the galactic heart of the universe, within the universe and within human energy field. When the music is heard, when the language is present, this field is naturally opened in both spheres, the human and the universal. These energy fields or centers then vibrate in harmony. This opens the gateway. This avails one of the opportunity to actually travel and exist within the Heart of the Goddess.

When certain aspects of the being open, the corresponding area of the universe vibrates its recognition. The frequencies become a gateway, as well as a personal acceleration. This language, once it continues to be spoken or sung, has an ever-moving, ever-changing effect. This is why we use the word dynamic. The effects or the results of this frequency, continue to expand the energy of the being present to them.

One can evolve to and travel within this area in life. Yet at this time, in human terms, there is a great opportunity to open oneself to the heart space of the Goddess without the seemingly endless training and evolutionary work that would normally have to be used. At this point in time, through the grace of the Goddess, Herself, beings are given the opportunity to actually step into this light without the training that is generally necessary.

The energy centers in the human body are often called chakras. There are seven major chakras located in ascending order from the base of the spine to the top of the head. Each energy center corresponds to a specific area in your body and in your energy field. Each chakra regulates, enhances and moves energy.

Generally in your world, the lower chakras are most active. The heart chakra remains the least developed. Even with people who are opening the higher centers, the heart chakra remains relatively undeveloped. The heart chakra is where the state of grace naturally unfolds. It is the fuller gateway to the upper chakras, in that once the heart chakra is opened, the upper gateways have a greater possibility of flow to carry the magnitude of being within.

The heart chakra is located in the center of the human body. If this is the central point in your body, then the resonance of this field carries energy above and below. If it is not fully functional, then energy flow is curtailed somewhere. As a result, one would not be wholly functional in all ways that can be expressed. So in developing this central chakra, the energy is fully available to all areas of the self. The endless universal flow is totally available. You can feel and know your connection to the Earth as well as to the Divine.

This is how it functions within the human body, but it also functions in a similar way in the outer spheres of existence. The Heart of the Goddess is the central point of space into which you can travel when you open your own heart, when you accelerate the center of your being. There are energy fields in the universe that correspond to the chakras within the energy body of the human. Therefore, when you expand the human central energy matrix, you have the availability of existing within the heart of the universe.

This is what the music, the language, the frequency of this system can do. It creates a compatible resonant frequency to the galactic heart of the universe within the human energy field. When Alawashka is heard, this field is naturally opened in both spheres, the human and the galactic. The fields or centers then vibrate in harmony. This harmonic opens the gateway. This opens the heart to the greater expression of love which avails one of the opportunity to actually travel and exist within the Heart of the Goddess. To open one's self to the Heart of the Goddess is to loosen the matrix of this human reality and open to a greater human reality.

This means that one can live in a fresh perspective. All the magic of the universe can dance within this space, for it is an endless expanse of generosity, blessing, harmony and freedom, which does not infringe on anything, ever. Each person, feeling the language within them, will be able to travel within this realm and exist fully. They will not experience individuality as separation or loss, but as the Divine expression of themselves. This is available to everyone that speaks, hears, or sings Alawashka. Whoever is in the presence of the vibration of Alawashka, even if they cannot hear, see or sing, will share in this blessing, healing and upliftment. This is the state of oneness that still contains singularity.

The gateways invite. The frequencies of this invitation are sent to those in harmony with the vibrational keys of the Galactic Heart Matrix, the Heart of the Universe. You open the gateways by vibrating to the blessed frequencies. This vibration provides you with the keys to the gateways.

The Galactic Heart Matrix is the main gateway for access to all the higher dimensional realms. There are many different levels or dimensional frequencies within this matrix. You will enter that which is most appropriate and beneficial to you. Each dimensional expression is highly refined. The energies and beings who reside in or travel to each dimensional expression of the matrix will be in harmonic resonance to you, as you will be to them.

By working with Alawashka you will begin to open the Galactic Heart Matrix, the Heart of the Goddess gateway and make it accessible on your world. As the gateway opens to you on your world it will, in time, be a beacon for other beings of Divine harmony to enter your world. These beings have been guides and teachers to many of you on this Earth. There are those who have been the guides to your guides. They have worked to bring the most refined energies and opportunities to humanity and the planet, and continue to do this. This sacred gateway opens the chambers of the highest frequencies of blessing and light. Many blessed unions take place within these realms.

As your experience and frequency acceleration grows, you will travel through the gateway and enter other gateways of expression. The gateway opened by Alawashka is what you may perceive as the front door. All other rooms, chambers and relationships of energy are accessed after you enter the front door. This realm is endless and bounteous.

PRESENCING ACCELERATION
The Invitation Within

A lawashka contains the highest vibrational frequencies. As we spoke of earlier, it helps each being raise their personal energy. It does this by very specialized methods. The gifts of these frequencies are multitudinous. The spiritual qualities provided can certainly entice you, and the benefits provided for you as an Earth being are equally profound. These Divine resonances can loosen and dissolve discordant energies.

Each being on this planet has had their share of pain and unresolved anger. Alawashka helps release patterns built when responding to those feelings and situations. This release alters the frequency again, and the Shollamaya Frequency continues its acceleration in concordance with each person. It also opens the being up to receive greater wisdom and understanding about the issues that created the feelings of discordance. I say it dissolves these energies, because the lower frequency of these vibrations are accelerated within the higher frequency.

Now, this is not necessarily the property of all higher frequencies. Many higher frequencies coexist with the lower, and go unnoticed until the being is raised to that higher frequency. This is a fail safe for access. With Alawashka, you are availed of the higher frequencies, because they are working on you to vibrate your energies to their highest expression. These frequencies resonate at a particular rate and in a particular code so that they continue to work.

By reading or singing one song or poem daily, you would make the energetic shifts it generally takes many years and sometimes centuries to make. I am not suggesting a discipline here. Setting aside a particular time or schedule can be convenient, if that is your inclination, but it is not necessary. Alawashka provides a durational matrix that creates newer patterns through the continued use over long periods of time. Presencing that energy is in a relationship of communion. You could listen to or read Alawashka daily or weekly. You could also read a song once, hold it dear to your heart and let the vibrational frequencies unfold as they will. By this communion, you are feeding the energy and you are accelerating its own dynamic quality within you.

These properties are built into this language. There is nothing for you to change within it. It is a process of letting the language carry you where you are already destined to be, and where part of you already exists. The dynamic quality of continual motion and change is already within the language. The acceleration and alignment is part of the language. This means there is very little to adjust to within the body. The frequency naturally goes to the highest level, augmenting all other energies within the being to do the same. It is the natural unfolding of the flower. It is the lotus of your heart. It is a gentle yet very powerful energy which does no harm at all. There is no major shift you have to get used to as in other systems of work. This will avail you of working in those other systems easily and more efficiently. It is for everyone.

By being with, speaking and reading Alawashka, these energies are easily assimilated into your being. It is not work. It is play. Speaking the poetry and singing the songs in Alawashka creates frequencies within you. It forms the Divine connection and keeps that covenant open. You do not have to continually work to access, practice, meditate, tune yourselves, have healings, and all the other things that have been necessary to you. This does not mean that you shouldn't do everything that you are called to do. It means, that finally, that which you seek is easily accessible.

In the past those who have sought the full connection to the All have had to leave cultures, family and home to break the "sleep" patterns that were upon them. The seers, the monks, the hermits, the witch in the wood, left society to break the isolation and control of the experiment. They brought you great religions, spiritual practices, healing practices and your alliance to the Divine. As chronology continued, they were also persecuted for these very same practices and visions.

You do not have to retreat to the hidden landscapes to bring the Divine into vision. Now, you can do this within your society. You may not have to create a new commune dedicated to the Goddess. Now, you can do this in the world because the shift is upon you and the energies are ready for your acceleration and evolution.

Alawashka makes this transition an easy, natural process. When you speak Alawashka, your connection to the Divine is in place. The gateways to the Divine are opened and you walk right in. There is no lag time. It is immediately enacted. Your highest frequencies are present. You encounter the highest of yourself, in communion with the Divine, and your connection is perfect. You will receive that which is the highest for yourself. You receive this in grace and ease. This is my nature. I am the language that initiated creation. I hold these exquisite frequencies within me, and accelerate each being in reverence and joy.

Personal experience with Alawashka is as varied as each individual. Some of you will feel immediate release. Some of you will feel spontaneous healing. Some of you will feel great joy. Some of you will dissolve old hurts. Some of you will have the impetus to change careers, move to another town or do more of what you have always wanted to do. This is how it can look on the outside, in the outer world.

Spiritually, you may notice different kinds of experiences. Some of you will feel the interdimensional shifts and recognize the new spheres and vibrational energies being accelerated. You may receive personal guidance. You may feel the flows of the universe. You may see Divine beings or travel through realms of great beauty and joy.

The vistas of the inner world are elegant and dynamic. Within your bodies and energy fields, a certain vibration becomes pronounced. Just as with a tuning fork, when you strike the fork, all frequencies of like nature start to vibrate. When you speak or read or sing in Alawashka, the tones of your soul and spirit vibrate at their highest natural inclination. Their natural inclination is to reverberate in concord with the Divine. Therefore, you begin to vibrate in harmony and connection with the Goddess, with the Divine energies of the universe as it occurs within you. Each of you has a personal frequency, and it sounds with the Divine. These frequencies are not always activated. Alawashka activates those oscillations, brings them into alignment and then accelerates their growth and rate of movement. This is the Shollamaya Frequency, the Goddess' Dynamic Resonant Frequency Accelerated Alignment, within Alawashka.

This process of activation is in continual motion. It does not dissipate or cease when you finish reading the language. It is a dynamic process. It persists, developing in activity. The activation accelerates, increasing in alignment and harmony to your greater connection and fulfillment. It augments how your energy resonates in yourself and in the world around you.

You are in perpetual expression of the universe and your Divine self. You are continuously augmenting this expression. You are ceaselessly accelerating your affinity to the Divine, which is seen as frequency, and this is always aligned and in balanced harmony. What Alawashka does, in certain practical terms, is create a personally specific field in which only the highest vibrations that you are working within are present. In this, the frequencies of limitation, isolation and fear are broken apart because they cannot maintain their integrity. They cannot sustain their holding pattern in this vibrational field. Just as a glass will shatter when certain notes and tones are played, the patterns of isolation and limitation will dissipate in the face of this higher frequency. While for my part, the creation and enactment of this process is a series of millions of complex associations and combinations done in one instant, on your part it is an immediate actualization.

In this acceleration, in this connection to the Divine, you are the one choosing. You have full freedom of choice to participate in your Divine connection or not. This is not done to you. This is a decision from your highest being to dance in the realms of the Divine, to be nurtured and to rejoice. You can sustain the acceleration and refinement by speaking Alawashka. To speak, hear or sing one song for one month, would expand your energies beyond your imagination.

As this oscillation is unfolding and accelerating, it is always taking into account your soul's greatest expression. It is always in harmony with your deepest relationship to the Divine. It is always working to honor you in the very personal expression of your focus and being. It will not accelerate you beyond what is comfortable and desirable to your nature. It will not force you to quicken beyond your capacities. It will not thrust you into any field, circumstances or feelings that you are not ready to receive, understand and implement.

This is how I am created to be. I am created for Divine connection, creation, unlimited possibilities and blessings. I am fully abundant in every sense you can imagine and beyond which you can know at the present time. In your relationship with me, Alawashka, you are linked to the Divine field of blessing and this is immediate and permanent. This is what you truly and fully desire in all of your being. This is what you have been seeking. You are all seeking to fully experience your personal link with and expression of the Divine.

You are cojoined to the All no matter what, but you do not experience this. I am the gateway of creation and when you participate with my energies you are indeed in creation, in augmentation, in the fullness of your capacity to be within the Divine. You consistently augment your capacities, your access, your fullness in every moment. This occurs instantaneously. Even with one encounter, one participation with Alawashka, you start this motion and it develops of its own accord, always in harmony with who you are.

Can you see what this means to yourself and to your world? Imagine that you are fully aware of your connection to the Goddess, to the blessings of the Universal All in every fiber of your being. Feel this connection. Feel the infusion, the augmentation of your energies. Sense the freedom to express divinity in every thought, in every motion, in every action of your life. Perceive the flow of life force, the swirl of galaxies moving within you. Let yourself be fully and unconditionally embraced by these expanding and encompassing energies, and savor this moment.

In this experience all the isolation disappears. All the fear disappears. You do not have to work to protect yourselves from harm or misfortune. You work because it is your nature and your fullness to express the Divine in every moment of existence on this planet and beyond. You do not need to control and demand. You do not need to defend. You celebrate your union to the Divine in the most joyful ways you can comprehend and expedite.

Imagine that each being on your planet is doing the very same thing. Imagine that your planet sings the songs and speaks the words that enact and empower this reciprocity in every moment of existence. Picture that each being, each person, is fully associated with the great All, and in this, they always think and act with honor and divinity. Each person is a precious gift bestowed to the world. See each being on this planet in full celebration of who they are. All of the sustenance and beauty of the universe is readily revealed and fully accessible. Each person is joyful in the expression of their blessings, and these blessings are constantly revealed. They act from their inner self, from their soul and spirit, and create wonders and beauty, always in harmony with their individual leanings and with the Universal All.

This is a portion of what I provide in my being, in my connection with the Goddess. This is what I am created to do. I joyfully celebrate my being. I am honored and pleased to be who I am, and that which I am, I give forth freely. I am here at this time to bring forth this blessing on your world. It is a gift for each of you.

Embracing Individual Expression
Welcoming the Focus

My appearance at this time is to give you the opportunity for direct access to creation within the highest energies of divinity and sublime balance. I am here to open your connection with the Divine and encourage your soul to create in joy, abundance, honor, love and blessing.

You can choose it all. You do not have to give up a method that works for you in order to create in Alawashka. Keep everything that works. There is no need to sacrifice your methods for those I bring forth. Enjoy them all. Engage in all those techniques that bring you joy and great fulfillment. You are Divine beings. You have lived under the spell of isolation, under the guise of separation from the Goddess, from the Heart of the Universe. You have been disengaged from your own divinity and from the greatest love. Alawashka opens and restores this relationship. I am here to restore your connection. I am here to reclaim the frequencies. I am here for blessing and creation. It is my nature. It is also yours.

Alawashka will help you reach your greatest potential as individuals and as a race of beings. In your world view, you consider that you have several races of beings on one planet. In actuality, you are one race of beings with different variations within that race. Just as you have different variations of skills and desires within any particular culture, you also have the same in your illusion of racial diversity. All humans are the same. In fact, all beings are inherently the same, in that all are created of the Divine Universal Oneness. We are all made of exactly the same energy. It is our focus, our inclinations towards creation and its expression, that appears to differentiate us all. Yes, there are beings with greater skills, with greater awareness. They can access the Divine energies with a fullness that is not within your energy framework at this time. This is what you are evolving toward.

You are all striving toward a greater expression of your soul and your access to the Divine. This is called Evolutionary Focus. Within this, each being has a particular focus that she or he is concerned with and wishes to experience. This is not destiny. Destiny is an agreement to participate in a specific series of events. Evolutionary Focus is the theme you have chosen to explore. It is the choice you made before you entered your present awareness in form. You have chosen a defined focus, a particular, specialized experience of your life here. You follow the thread which you created, and express yourself in that motif.

Personal Frequency is an energetic force that is in tune with the individual collective vibrations one sends out. There are frequencies of energy that live or exist to augment the understanding of individual beings through evolutionary focus. When one works on one's own growth and does so with honor, then certain expanded frequencies are available. This creates a spiraling effect.

A person is working within a particular frequency at any given moment, which is their personal vibration traveling along their evolutionary focus. Then, something new occurs. Perhaps they see something in a new way or have been working on a particular energy and something new enters their field. If this individual is willing to work with this newness, and gain insight and understanding, that frequency will shift.

Something new is always happening. There are always many opportunities to encompass greater growth and higher frequencies. This need not occur in just the spiritual sense. One can look at any occurrence and bring the wisdom of being to it. This will change the qualities and the frequencies. Humans do this all the time. When someone new comes into your life, your frequency changes. When new opportunities are taken and explored, your frequency changes. When a new idea or a new way of thinking comes forth, your frequency changes. It is up to the individual whether they gain the resonance of that frequency and sustain it. Sustaining the frequency requires adapting one's life and one's thought to this new way of being, seeing and thinking. The assertion that a person has "fallen back on his old ways" means that although the new frequency was available for this person, he could not sustain it and returned to the previous frequency.

Higher frequencies are generally achieved when something new is added and one adapts to that newness. Through the inner exploration and outer experiences, one is availed of opportunities for frequency shifts. Either one can sustain the new frequency or one returns to the more familiar frequency. There are frequencies that tend to have a greater hold on certain people. What you would consider a negative frequency has a stronger pull to some people. It becomes like a mud they are stuck in and cannot break free. The higher frequencies tend to be more open, yet they also require a certain amount of maintenance work within them so the being can continue to grow and develop.

I speak of all this to lay another level of groundwork for you. To access the frequencies of this language was once a very difficult thing. Very few people could return to the higher frequency once the human factor and the Earth relationship was altered to a lower frequency. Yet, at this time, in your days, the language has returned of its own free choice to avail you of the frequencies it holds. This means you have immediate access to what once was a process of development.

Now, in this moment, you can access the frequencies of wisdom and harmony. This language generates a great many frequencies. Each word, each collection of words, how they are used and what they express gives off a frequency. At times with several words strung together in a sentence, each word compounds the others and radiates a newer frequency than the individual words can do alone. In this way, words in Alawashka have several and varied meanings which are related to the other words that surround them. This changes the frequency, whether slightly or considerably.

Alawashka works with those systems within yourself that are intuitive and coincidental. They are all part of the same system. It is always a matter of attention. When you begin to work with Alawashka, you may have more coincidences in your life. Become aware of those messages. Recognize the synchronicity of thoughts and events. This is a good way to recognize what you are accessing, and what changes are developing through working with the language.

Reading the language and being in its resonant field is what generates these shifts. You may already be experiencing these changes. Some of these shifts in awareness may start to occur while reading this book. My name is a name of frequency and you may experience these accelerations as you read, because you have shifted your vibrational awareness into the fields I am speaking from. Alawashka can initiate the vibrational resonance to help you shift your being. It may begin when you read this book and gain the sweetness of those shifts simply by entering the fields I provide through this text. You may choose to participate in the words, language and music by more direct means. These frequencies are available for you.

As you participate, you may start to feel connections or be aware of associations that have escaped you before. You may find that you have always wanted to start a new business, and now you are thinking about it more than ever. Notice this. Something is changing here. You may realize that you are not getting as upset by situations that normally trigger you. You may be present to a fear that has been long-standing, yet so deep you could not see it. You may feel a freedom that you have not felt in a long time. Notice it. I relate these experiences in practical terms so that you can see the many different ways Alawashka can help you shift into the greater expression of your being. There are many energetic changes that occur, and for most people these are subtle. Alawashka works in the practical world as well as the spiritual, for creation exists in all worlds and dimensions. All these experiences, and so many more that you will discover, exemplify consistent changes in your frequency and signs of what you are working with.

Many people have a very rich dream life wherein they do a significant amount of work. You may be augmenting your own field through your dreams. Your dream patterns may change to reveal greater understanding and communication. This is another way to gather evidence of your changing inner dynamic.

There are instances of dramatic and remarkable transformations working with Alawashka. Healing has occurred instantaneously. Changes in life patterns have opened immediately. Great insights occur in a moment and transform that person forever. This is possible. This is very possible. More importantly, your energy is shifting and aligning to your greatest expression of self. Sometimes that is very subtle. It is beneficial to be aware of the subtle changes that are unfolding in small ways. These generally make up a very large picture.

Another important aspect of Alawashka is that certain aspects of your life will gracefully fall away. These are the thoughts, events and people that are no longer able to vibrate in the same field of experience that you are holding. As Alawashka increases your abilities to hold higher and higher vibrational rates and frequencies, those parts of your life that are unaccustomed to and uncomfortable in higher vibrations will appear to vanish.

The alterations in your personal field, created through Alawashka, are a relationship of sound and light that moves you into higher levels of experience. A lower frequency is a denser format or pattern of vibration. It is lower and slower. It attracts certain situations, thoughts and energies. These can occur for humans as uncomfortable emotions, or situations which seem futile, unyielding and repressive. A higher frequency is more open and progressive. Your field would be vibrating at a faster rate. You would be shaking up and shaking away the perceived limitations for more freedom and joy. This actually sets up an energetic barrier to those experiences that were previously restrictive. Experiences, situations and thoughts will work the same way. You may notice that certain situations are no longer important to you or that certain thoughts of insecurity or fear are not coming into play at the same rate as before. This is all due to the dynamic change in your ability to hold and participate in the acceleration of your personal field into a higher frequency.

You may not want to chart the changes in your energy. You may feel that the changes are occurring, and that will be enough for you. I have provided these short examples, just to help you notice some of the possible areas of change. Whether you notice these aspects of change or not, your energetic modifications will continue to augment and unfold. Through the sequence of time, you will gather greater strength, energy and joy in your life. If you have held onto certain patterns, fears or thoughts, these may be very prominent in your thoughts initially. If this is the case, know that you are releasing these patterns, and that your Divine self feels it is most important for you to follow the threads of these thoughts and patterns to their release. That will be the reason they feel particularly prominent for you. Most often, the energies you raise will simply release what is no longer appropriate for your soul. In the resonant frequencies of Alawashka, these old patterns can just go. For many, this is what occurs. They do not notice any specific change, save for the subtle feeling that they are more happy, more healthy and have greater freedom to express themselves.

As your energy shifts, ever expanding into its highest expression, many things are efficiently melted away. Many things you would normally have to process and resolve through all the methods you presently use, would merely dissolve into the higher frequency. Issues about family and guilt and victim and such, would melt away. Their energies would be resolved in greater understanding. You would notice what was there, and it would resolve itself by the nature of the frequency you are employing in the language.

CREATING GRACEFUL ACCELERATION
Individuals and Groups

The Alawashka language is created so that each person who encounters it has their personal frequency vibrating at an elevated rate that is compatible with their own being and development. The changes that occur are compatible with each individual. The frequency sent from Alawashka starts to alter in direct relationship with the person who is hearing or speaking the language. This means, that although the language and its significance will be understood, each individual's energies will be changing at different rates, times and frequencies. The language generates infusions which, on their own, work within the individual.

Within a group, a different energy is also created. The collected frequencies find a particular level for the whole group. In this way the group forms a base, and then the frequencies elevate within the group and also within each individual. What may interest you about the oscillation within a group speaking Alawashka is that the highest frequency available creates the base energies for the whole group experience.

Generally speaking, group work is as effective, at least initially, as the lowest frequency working. Without Alawashka, when ritual is performed, or a group meditation is convened, the highest energy of any one individual within the group decreases to accommodate the lowest energy of any one person working in the group. The higher energy may still be working within the individual person who can bring it forth, but the lowest energy is what creates the group dynamic. The person with the high vibrational rate may create doorways or corridors to bring frequencies in, or call in forces and beings to work within the group, but the result is the same.

The Alawashka language is different. It raises the entire group to the highest frequency that can be sustained by any one individual. This means that the highest frequency of any one person can be experienced by all people within that group. The highest, most refined frequency is provided. It becomes the platform from which the group may choose to resonate. This is the base from which the entire process begins. This energetic cohesion then raises all frequencies to the highest expression.

Later, each individual works with whatever energy level they can to ensure comfort and efficiency. Some people within that group may continue on the higher frequency. Others may return to a different frequency. They may return to the frequency with which they are used to working. If that is the case, the energies of the group and the highest expression will still be present and available to them when they are ready to integrate it. An individual may be ready to integrate a higher frequency in the moment. If that is the case, it will be done and their frequency will be raised by the energies they have chosen.

This highest resonant field is not the fullness of the group experience. The individual generating the highest frequency will naturally be availed of even higher frequency experiences. This individual can accelerate at a much faster and more graceful rate. The frequencies can increase vibrational rate indefinitely. These greater dimensional textures and patterns will be available to the individual and, naturally, to the group.

All the Alawashka frequencies are aligned with the individual. I am always aware of your personal frequency, evolutionary focus and the myriad of energetic streams involved. You will not get overstimulated or out of alignment by this work, unless you are looking for that or require it for specific purposes. The energies generated resonate to your personal frequency and bring that to you in a newly aligned format. This is the process of evolution within Alawashka. It is gentle and profound. The energies will raise your comfort level. You will be able to be comfortable with more things, greater changes, and higher levels of frequency because the energies are all aligned with you, specifically and directly, taking into account every aspect of your being.

The dynamic energies of the language and its many frequencies is in continual expansion. Its dynamics continue to augment the existing intentions and energies of those in contact with the language, and avails them of the opportunity to grow with great speed towards higher personal evolution.

The workings of the language can be associated with a system of tuning forks. Each being has a frequency that they exist within. This frequency is actually a collection of many frequencies which create one specific frequency vibration inclusive of its harmonics. The language, Alawashka, becomes the tuning fork for the highest frequency working within the individual. As with a tuning fork, once the frequency is struck, the same frequency is activated and vibrates within the individual. If a tuning fork is struck on the note A, all of the A notes will resonate. This creates a compatible resonant field in which all frequencies of like nature answer the call of the A note.

When an individual participates with the language, the highest frequency of their being is struck. This resonates their being to reach that high frequency and aligns them with the highest expression of that vibration. This means that the best of you, your highest aspirations, your greatest love, your most profound visions are fully present, alive and activated. In the most optimal expression of this activation, the individual will hold that frequency and the lower energies will raise to that level on what you may call a permanent basis. The whole of being becomes a compatible resonant field for the experience of their highest frequency.

When this occurs, the individual is availed of even higher frequencies. The highest frequency that was experienced now creates an opening in the resonant field for even higher frequencies to be expressed. With continual contact with the language of Alawashka, one is availed of the highest possible frequencies for the human, and great contact with the highest possible frequencies of being. Again, this is always aligned with the unique purpose of the individual. There are peaks and levels that occur within the frequency ranges. One assimilates the newer frequency, works in that energy, accesses the dimension of that frequency and, then, as the peak of that vibration is reached, it grows open to the next resonant alignment.

What generally occurs in personal growth and evolution is that the frequency is already present, yet it needs to be struck and activated for its fullness to come forth. When a person encounters something new that "strikes a chord" within them, what occurs is the activation of a frequency within them. The individual works with that energy and either accepts it and infuses it into their being or does not. If not, the resonance of the person returns to their average frequency. If they do accept it, then the higher frequency becomes completely activated and they alter their energy pattern. This is what occurs on a daily basis for humans.

With Alawashka, the highest frequency is singled out. It is not a semi-random meeting of beings or thoughts that begins the activation. A specific chord within the person, which vibrates to the highest level they can access at that time, is singled out and activated. This creates an immediate opportunity for that person to use this frequency to the highest and fullest expression possible. Once this is in place, the process continues. As I mentioned, this is dynamic, which means it is continually activated. If one cannot hold the higher frequency, then there is release. One can always return to the highest frequency, once again, and infuse that vibration more successfully. Even if the person or being cannot hold or sustain the frequency, an alteration occurs allowing for that frequency to be more stabilized within the individual.

Alawashka accelerates that process both individually and collectively. What may evolve in several years, can evolve in weeks or days, and in some cases, in the moment. Those who have participated in Alawashka rituals have felt immediate results, even from only one experience. There have been healings in one moment that were persistent health complaints. There have been openings within people that have changed their lives to greater beauty and joy. There have been people who have truly fallen in love, have created the careers they always wanted, have gained release and insight into their personal limitations and more. Those who are more specifically aware of the vibrational qualities and realms have been transported to levels that hold great beauty and purpose. The list of these occurrences is innumerable.

All these experiences and shifts are also possible within a group. Each collection of individuals within a group speaking, listening to, or reading Alawashka, becomes activated to the highest frequency possible for any individual within that group. This may or may not be sustained for all, but it is activated within each individual. Imagine, as an example, that meditating with a highly evolved person, a great teacher, a wise woman, would bring you to the frequency of that person. Imagine the acceleration and leap that would make within you. You would be availed of that high energy frequency for the time you are with them. You would also have the opportunity to raise your frequency to that level and sustain it, if that were in line with your life and purpose. The possibility is astounding.

This exchange is reciprocal. By vibrating to that extraordinary frequency, you would be availing the teacher of the opportunity to expand even further. You would be helping to create the base and sustain that, which then creates the platform for energies to accelerate even further.

These Divine frequency accelerations occur when participating with this language. This process expands within a group because all the highest energies desire to resonate with each other. A symphony of high frequencies takes place. One portion of the frequency remains consistently activated. Another portion, which I will for the moment term the holding frequency, has the potential to be continually activated. It is not activated in full until the individual can hold that energy. If the being can hold the energy, then it is engaged. If not, then it remains held in potential until the being can comfortably do this. If a group of three people speaks the poetry of Alawashka together, the vibrations of the highest frequency of those three people will be activated. If each can sustain this energy, then they will be fully aligned and hold this energy on a permanent basis. Permanent, for this discussion, is still very much in flux. Their contact with others in a similar vein will create the highest energy within that group. It accelerates exponentially.

Imagine a group of thirty people speaking or listening to the language and being aligned with the highest frequency. They have an amazing access to their highest potential, and they have access to the highest frequency of all who are gathered. In this case every one of those thirty people would be resonating to the highest frequency available to any of them. Each person would be raising their vibrational rate to the highest resonating energy and working at that level. In accord with this, the whole group becomes instantly aligned with this frequency. It is a group field that is generated and sustained within the time allotted for the ritual experience. This is a multidimensional experience.

The highest vibration has access to resonate at an even higher level. This can be accomplished in many different ways, but using the example of one individual in the group, as mentioned previously, if the highest vibration of that one person is filled with the oscillation of that experience, she or he can lift to the next frequency ratio. The group will naturally be availed of that new level, as well.

The vibrational effect is exponential, meaning it multiplies by a higher sequence. The exponential results of 5 people working together equals the effects of 3,125 people working at the highest frequency level available to any one person in the group. In this situation the power and energy raised by a small group would have the effect of many. Therefore, the expansion of these frequencies would encompass a broader field. This field then generates a higher degree of refined frequency through a wider expanse.

Six people working with Alawashka would generate the reverberations of 46,656 people resonating to their highest possible frequency for each and sending this forth into the universe. Eight people would generate the power of 16,777,216 people. The energy generated by a group of eight people would be expressed by the highest frequency of any one person communing in Alawashka and working with the intensity of 16,777,216 people at the highest level. That is the combined energy of a large city area or perhaps even a country.

If there are ten people in the group, the exponential force is 10,000,000,000. The acceleration of frequency resonating in the ritual is as though 10 billion people were holding the highest vibrational rate possible to those collected. So, the effect is as if nearly double entire populous of the Earth were all raising their vibrations and intentions to the highest possible factors and joyfully sending out this energy. This in itself is exceedingly dramatic.

As mentioned previously, sustaining that level of vibrational excellence is a matter of individual resonance. Yet the vast access to healing, cleansing and global communion would have the direct potential to alter and elevate the course of human relationships. The flow of blessings spread across your world, in just one hour, could send waves of joyous healing and Divine spiritual essence moving through every particle on and within Gaia. Every person, every animal, every tree, every grain of sand would be washed and blessed. Gaia is tuned to these frequencies and has the power, grace and means to hold these energies.

If we increase the number of people in that group to the thirty people mentioned in the original example, then the exponential results of thirty people singing Alawashka in ritual is 6.176733962 to the 45 power or

6,176,733,962,000,000,000,000,000,000,000,000,000,000,000,000. This is the amount of energy that can be raised by a totally conscious galaxy of beings. This number is beyond comprehension and more than can be counted, but it can show you the incredible expansion powers of these blessings.

This energy, as extreme as the mathematics appear, will not blast you off of the planet. You will not go circling into multidimensional space. Your individual energy resonance is already designed to hold these frequencies for your highest blessing. Each of you will hold what is appropriate for your own being. Everyone on the planet would dip into the pool of Divine nectar and drink their fill. Each person's expansion, healing and joyful spiritual acceleration would raise according to their highest benefit. And this powerful yet subtle energy would be available even if it a song were sung only once by thirty people.

While this energy may not be able to be sustained by all of the people, many more of the people would be able to sustain it. Very importantly, many more people would be able to sustain their highest level of personal frequency. The resonant field, which is in dynamic perpetual motion, would help each person hold their highest frequency pattern and continue to raise the vibrations as a collective unit for all.

Imagine what would take place if people all over your planet were speaking this language to each other. Even if they used one phrase in Alawashka as a greeting, the frequency of the whole planet would be accelerated to the highest energy of any one individual. If in greeting, **"Shalka Matista,"** "I celebrate the pathways of Divine flow," were spoken, the sacred communion of energies would indeed be uplifted and flow to all.

This acceleration of frequency and change in awareness occurs on the personal level, creating effects directly related to one person's experience. If you multiply this experience by many people, you are then working on the planetary level. Perhaps it will reach into the darkness of closed minds and open people to the beauty that is already present waiting for them to notice and cultivate within their hearts. Perhaps the lives of each one will be altered by the honoring energy that this language is. Perhaps the beauty of life will unfold into each heart and transform the perceived differences into an appreciative pursuit of unique discovery. Perhaps an Alawashka song will be played in the United Nations. Perhaps with these blessings the nations who see only discordant differences in politics and beliefs will see those differences within the qualities of honor and love. Perhaps the plants will flourish with the language spoken and sung to them. Perhaps the waters will once again run clear when they hear the blessings of this music. Perhaps each life will be enriched by the recognition of the Sacred Divinity within. Perhaps all beings will have fun and joy and celebration within all moments of their lives. Perhaps you will all intend that this is so.

Imagine societies creating themselves anew by singing or speaking the poems of opening. Imagine the dynamic frequencies, moving and vibrating to higher and higher levels, giving new insights to social and family relationships built on honor, love and truth. Imagine the mechanisms of society built in harmony with the planet so that once again, the planet fulfills Herself and supports you, while you are fulfilling yourselves and supporting Her.

As Alawashka comes into greater use, in personal ceremony, in group celebration and later, spoken in language, the individual and the whole society shifts awareness and opens to dimensions that seemed to be less accessible or perhaps not even present. If it were only this that occurred, it would still have major repercussions on your planet. Yet this is a small portion of what can occur.

Prolonged experience with the language would assure that those frequencies would hold, and this would indeed raise the level of energy for the whole planet. Because this is a dynamic process, there is continued growth and acceleration. The higher energies continually seek to resonate with even higher frequencies. The vibrations become finer and clearer. This works on individuals and on the collective of beings in this planet. There is no end to the heights this frequency alignment can attain. Not all of them may be fully experienced in the body, but they can be attained.

The language also beneficially alters the planet, Herself. She, too, accelerates Her energies for the highest frequencies of Her being. That is part of the great shift that is occurring at this time. The planet is vibrating at a different frequency. The energetic patterns of this planet are in a new alignment. The frequencies and interdimensional properties of Her vibrational grid have moved to a much higher level than previous to this time. She is evolving. Alawashka is a language that She knows in Her stone and Her bone. Gathering together to speak Alawashka to Her, will aid in Her personal growth and evolution as well as your own.

When working with the energies of this planet, it is important to ask Her what She wants. It is not always in Her best interest to attempt to stabilize Her energies. She may want to explode with vibrational joy and expansion. She may want to shift into accelerated blessing. Ask Her. When you send Her energy, send it free of attachment. Send it for Her to access Her highest energies in beauty and freedom.

When you speak Alawashka to Her, to Gaia, do it as an honoring gift. Send Her the beauty and freedom and energy to do what She wants with it. Singing the poems to Her will also augment the energies of the planet, the elementals, the plant and animal life, the humans and other beings on this planet, and the greater energies of the atmosphere and beyond. This language is not confined to the Earth realm. It is the language of creation from the Heart of the Universe. It is spoken in other planets, and is known in many more. Beings from many systems are waiting for all of you to speak Alawashka.

I Alawashka, wanted to take the time to explain these aspects of Alawashka in a fuller sense so each of you could see the benefits of this language. So that you could understand, in a fuller sense, the properties and changes within it. These properties are already within your personal growth pattern which the language lovingly augments in a continual event, which we call life.

THE DANCE OF NOW
Choosing the Gifts

In this period of time on Earth, many beings have come to Earth to experience this amazing sequence of events. This sequence of events is the great shift in the energies and possibilities of this planet. Each life, each human is engaged in a focus within the whole of this planet. Each has come to experience and to live a life within the certain guidelines you created before your birth. Now, each of you had some coaching from a team of beings who helped you develop your game plan. For example, you may have decided to be born into a particular social background, religion or race. That was one decision. You may have selected a specific theme, like science or music or psychology. You chose certain goals. These goals are levels of experience and not levels of success.

If you determined that you were going to experience the nature of a loving partnership on this planet, then whether you have been married for twenty years or have had several intense but short relationships, your goal would be accomplished in this area. These are certain guidelines for your life that you intended before incarnation.

You are continually evolving in your expression of life. You are making changes in your choices, based on what you are experiencing and learning. The decisions and conclusions you made before you came into body are in constant revision because of your growth and development. You are fully able to refine, enhance and change your experience and expression of being in every moment. When you elected to be here, you were also aware of the timelines and the general trends of this chronological period. You volunteered to come at this time, because of the intensity of this timeline experience.

The world is going through an amazing change. Your planet is changing Her form in more dramatic ways than have been experienced in quite some time. This is an incredible joy and exhilaration for Her. Those people who plot the Earth's changes can show there are more earthquakes, eruptions, storms, floods, temperature variations and the like, than in any time frame that has been noted. While this may or may not be accurate, the joy and expansion of Terra Gaia is very present and active. She is delighting in this remarkable growth and a vast array of beings are collecting to celebrate this new and profound awakening. These beings are gathering from the interdimensional realms to help bring in and anchor the new frequencies She is integrating.

Terra Gaia is a Goddess. She is a creator. She is an alive, aware being with immense capacity. She births beings. Open your eyes to whom is providing your world. She, by the grace of Her joy and unbounded love, has created a world that is rich and beautiful. She delights in and cherishes each of you. These changes upon Her and within Her are a new exploration that She has invited you to attend. Each of you has freely and joyfully accepted that invitation. This celebration is also your celebration.

Moreover, the changes in your societies since your World War Two, have changed what humans think of as being human. You are fully aware of each other. You have greater extremes now. You have come here to experience these extremes. These extremes are polarities that accentuate streams of energy into a dynamic exchange. Because of these extremes, you have the opportunity to participate in the freedom and growth of your being. These extremes clearly show you avenues of participation. While you may have judgments about it being easy for you to live in these extremes, you are here to expand your inner being into the full connection to the Divine. You are recreating humanity. You have also come to help the evolution of this planet and all beings upon it, including yourselves, to rise beyond the harshness of the extremes and to open to the grace of being. You chose to be here for all of it.

You are here to participate in the most unusual event in universal awakening. You will help with the greatest acceleration and interdimensional experience. This event, the evolution of your planet, your world and naturally yourselves, will reverberate throughout the cosmos in a dance of ever-unfolding magnitude and grace. The acceleration of your world, of your reality, will also accelerate the whole of the cosmos. Can you not see how cherished you all are to us? Your lives, your presence, your unfolding is an access point for all consciousness everywhere.

Choosing to experience the extremes and choosing to experience your connection to the Divine within this specialized focus is a worthy endeavor for any being. You will do this in your own way, which is given to you by the experiences you have engaged in. You have also, for the most part, chosen to do this within your societies. You are teachers, doctors, students and parents. You are voters and politicians. You are all trades, all colors, and all preferences. You are doing this in your way. You have many opportunities for help. These opportunities are awakening within you and outside of you. Some of them are part of your being, other opportunities are gifts from above.

One of your own gifts is your innate intuition. You hear messages all the time that guide you in your decisions and help you find the best path for your expression and experience. Some of you pass off Divine providence and creation as coincidence. Your cultural definition views coincidence in a depreciated, derisive manner. Coincidence is a remarkable concurrence of corresponding events, be this event an action or a thought. One may think of it as a curiosity and treat it quite offhandedly, but it is an affirmation of your ability to connect with the universe in an immediate and direct fashion.

In one sense, you have created this event to correspond to another. This event or circumstance is dramatic enough to attract your attention to the correspondence.

Be aware of these correspondences and you will sense the greater guidance that is there for you. Sometimes you are the one providing your own guidance. You have reached beyond the sequential timelines into the probable future and, through agreement, have created a situation to call your attention to something. Sometimes the coincidence is orchestrated for you, to bring your attention to the Divine guidance that is present. This is not to be passed off. The more you notice, the more often it will occur, and more guidance and intuition will help you in your life.

Some of you will be experiencing new levels of your intuitive processes. All the legends and stories of remarkable gifts are presently opening for you at this time. You may learn to commune with the animals. You may perceive others' distress and be able to help them. You may feel the strong guidance within to take or avoid certain actions. These are your gifts. If you are interested in learning from others in these regards, there are teachers with great expertise. These gifts will evolve within you, and naturally there are those who can help your level of clarity and expertise. Use your gifts to the best of your abilities. They are a natural expression of your divinity and your connection to the Divine Source of All.

Another innate gift is your feeling about things. This is not an emotional response, yet you feel it in a sensory way. You know when something does not feel right. You know when you get a warning. You also know when something feels very right. Many of you tend to pass off these experiences as well. You second guess yourselves, or give a person or a situation "the benefit of the doubt." *There is no benefit when you doubt your innate and inner understanding of a situation and favor the logical, objective approach.* These feelings convey a message. Pay attention to the message. These impressions are a personal guidance system. Listening to the messages you receive and acting upon them is a choice that you make to remember your Divine connection and act within that choice.

All these gifts - your intuition, your feelings, your dreams, your coincidental connections - are a personal guidance system which is in synchronicity to the Divine and to your being. When you are in life's circumstances these are guides for your personal choices. When you are offered advice or connect with energies you are not familiar with, these inner prompting will bring you to a greater clarity. You are here to use everything in the joyful dance of evolutionary unfolding. Your innate discernment and impressions augment your life.

I say this in regard to my own messages to you, as well. If what I convey does not resonate with you, then trust yourself before you trust me. In all things, trust yourself. You are the access to the Divine. The presence of the Goddess is firmly within you. If you are prompted by inner clarity to follow a dream or an inner urging, do so knowing that you are following your inner guidance. If you are uncomfortable with a message or a connection, no matter where it comes from, no matter which person or Divine being you are communicating with, trust your own knowing first. When you do this, you honor your Self. You honor the Divine gift of being and consciousness that you are.

THE KEEPERS OF ALAWASHKA
Who Have Gone Before, Come Again

A t one time Alawashka was only used for sacred ritual. There were people and beings here who still held the language. Some of these people were human and held the vibration for humanity. They have incarnated here many times to hold those frequencies in readiment for this age.

Some of those beings were not inherently human, but have birthed into the human form to understand the complexity of being human. They did this to interdimensionally hold this language and frequency for this time. I shall call them the Keepers.

The Keepers continued to speak Alawashka, but in more secret ways. They worked with humanity to continuously reinforce the opening that Anshara provided. This eventually developed into schools of wisdom. These schools of wisdom developed into tribes of peoples. Within those tribes who journeyed this planet, Alawashka was the secret tongue. It was spoken secretly in sacred ritual. The teachings of being and the universe were spoken, sung and enacted. These rituals became ritual schools for initiated people. Much of the language has been totally lost, yet in some of the older languages you will find words that are direct descendants of Alawashka.

As time continued on this plane, and more and more of the wisdom had to be secret, the schools became smaller and smaller. They became very hidden. It became the charge of the women to hold the energies and the secrets. Females, by nature, can hold energy within for sustained periods of time. There is no fault in the nature of male or female. Both men and women are of glory. This is a way of helping you to understand the language. Many secret societies of women spoke some Alawashka in their rituals and rites. The women held this language as long as they could. With the wars and the power struggles, the women s societies were wiped out. The language was nearly lost. Some words had been incorporated into other languages as memory triggers, but the beauty and energy of the language could not be sustained.

Now, at this time, some of the Keepers, are returning to you. A Keeper works with a very special containment field to help hold and embody specific wisdom, energetic activations, frequencies and patterns to be employed at the right time. There are various levels and expression of Keepers. Some hold portions of the language and speak its variations. Some hold certain frequencies, yet are not present to the music. Each holds what is right for them, birthed into their being to bring it forth at this time.

You need not be a Keeper to know me in your hearts, to lift the veils of forgetfulness and touch the language that was spoken and sung long ago. I am a universal presence, sung in the cells of beingness. You need not aspire to channel me or retrieve messages directly from me in order to commune with me. Communion is already done. I am here to kiss your foreheads in annointment and waken you from slumber into the morning. The songs and rituals here in this book and those which will come in the next, will brush the sleep from your eyes and the longing from your heart.

Lumari is the only true full Keeper of Alawashka on this planet and beyond. She is that which holds the fullness of my being and language for this world and many worlds beyond. She is the breath of my breath. She has come to bring Alawashka out into the open on Earth in a very direct manner.

She has reclaimed the language in its fullness and retrieved the specific rituals to be shared in this day. She has shared these rituals with others and has begun this phase of the journey that is hers. She holds the initiation rites within. She has also reclaimed the soul songs.

Soul songs are the poems in Alawashka that each person s greatest spirit longs to sing. Each song is a unique expression of that being or person and their greatest joy and connection. As you read your soul song in Alawashka you continually create the divinity that is your true expression.

Lumari, as the Keeper, is bringing forth the language to be spoken once again on this planet. The poems in this book are sacred songs that were sung in the hidden temples. They were sung and spoken to bring in the blessings for those involved and for their family, community and this world. These songs are returned to you now for the opening of Divinity.

As you participate with the songs and practices that follow, you are restoring, renewing and rededicating your lives in blessing. May you be filled with the waters of the Divine.

I am the Gateway to the Galactic Matrix.
Let the portals open wide.
Let your singing hearts rejoice.

ENGAGING THE BLESSINGS

A s you have learned, the frequencies of Alawashka are endlessly varied. They work with your own vibrational resonance and help you expand to your next level of personal growth. There are many ways to participate with Alawashka. I have included certain songs to introduce you to these blessed streams. Each poem has a unique focus. Each is a full connection to the Divine.

You can use them in any way that occurs to you. Do not limit your creativity by my suggestions. Your exploration, your discovery and your methods are honored. We, Lumari and I, provide these aspects for you to experience and explore.

The most simple way to work with Alawashka is to read one of the songs. Whether you read aloud or in silence is a matter of preference. By reading the words, the frequencies unfold. One song can be used as a morning or evening recitation. Upon awakening or retiring you could read one of these songs to set the tone of your day or activate those energies while you sleep. I do suggest that you allow yourself some time to experience the energies as you read, and reflect upon the shifts once you finish.

You could have someone else read to you, and both of you would be in the expression of your connection to the Divine All, and this would be activated in the moment. This does not exclude those who cannot physically hear or read or who have any other perceived physiological disability. The language

Alawashka is a vibration and frequency and in and of itself, it creates. Even if you could not hear, could not think, could not perceive, you would still be augmented.

Meditation with Alawashka provides the time and dimensional embrace for a fuller experience. By singing or speaking a song in Alawashka, then meditating along and with these frequencies, you can clearly feel the shifts. This avails you of the opportunity to work with the frequencies and accelerate your vibrational resonance in a greater manner. You would naturally choose the time that provides you with the space and freedom to explore the unfolding of higher dimensional resonance and the grace to be as you need.

You may also choose to participate in an Alawashka practice. While Lumari creates these rituals in person, we have created one for you in this book. Before you decide to participate, read it to see whether it delights and intrigues you. These practices create a fuller experience of the language because they are created to hold specific formats of frequency in specific patterns to aid your inner transitions.

Any method you choose is appropriate for you. All will proceed in grace and honor of your being.

To experience a small taste of my frequencies, before we begin working directly with an Alawashka format, we shall open a bit of the gateway for you. Please, sit back and relax yourself in the manner in which you are most comfortable.

- ◆ Take a slow deep breath.
- ◆ Feel the breath rise and fall within you.
- ◆ Take another deep breath.
- ◆ Imagine that this breath is a long shimmering thread that extends from the Heart of the Universe to you.
- ◆ Take another slow deep breath and feel this thread, which is permeated with light, joy, and sparkling energies, fill you with the grace of being.
- ◆ Take ten slow deep breaths, and with each breath, feel yourself being filled, being nurtured, being honored and being loved by the being you most often refer to as god or goddess. Sense the blessings that they offer you.

Listen for the words that may come to you.
♦ Now take ten more slow deep breaths.
♦ Feel the frequencies I am sending you right now.
♦ Feel the interconnectedness of Divine blessing. Feel it flow to you and within you.
♦ Feel and connect with the great joy, love and blessing that is the natural state of being in the universe and within yourself.
♦ Close your eyes. Feel the flow from the Heart of the Goddess gently touching you and encouraging you to know a deeper, more beautiful part of your being. When you are ready, open your eyes.

ALAWASHKA PRACTICE

There are many ways to work with this language. Trust your heart and creativity to explore the many possibilities. I have some suggestions for its work to help you start the process. The following Alawashka songs are written in Alawashka with the phonetic pronunciation and an English translation.

Musical notations for two songs are included. If you hear your own melody for a poem or song, please engage it. It may very well be the melody your heart wants you to sing.

I have selected certain song/poems that have an energetic ratio that is most pleasing and special. I include information and descriptions of the frequencies for your understanding. You may choose to recite one poem for a time and explore that experience. I have included poems for recitation as well as for song.

You may want to create your own personal ritual or meditations, using the poems as part of work you would like to do, or incorporate them in work you already do. All of this is wonderful. Choose the exploration that calls to you and delights you.

These explanations and guidelines are provided for your personal exploration. They are not rules of propriety. I have noticed that creating a special format for celebration often provides the richest and most concentrated expression. Find your own rhythms within.

In creating a personal experience of practice with Alawashka, you may want to set the space into which it will unfold. Setting the space is the process of clearing the energy and creating a moment in time to do sacred work. Then the expression of your intention is clear, and you act to set your intention. Your intention is the purpose of the ritual.

To create a personal ritual for Alawashka, you would create a clearing to work with a particular poem, to infuse its energies within your being. Quiet, undisturbed time that is set aside for your personal expression is ritual.

You may create your own personal ritual or meditation with Alawashka. If you already have a special method or procedure for connecting with Divine energies, use that to set the space. You may then work with the Alawashka song of your choice. Include your personal methods of setting sacred space, and calling forth those energies that are most beneficial to you. You can invite your guides, if you work with them, or create a space that is very intimate and personal. You can bring your sacred tools. You can dance; you can laugh; you can sing.

Alawashka is a celebration of personal and universal joy and abundance. All energies and forms who hold this frequency, who hold you in love, honor and truth, are invited to play. It is always, always your choice in what you create, who you invite and what you decide to bring. It is not necessary to create ritual, as Alawashka creates space by its very nature, yet this joyful expression of ritual is always welcomed.

You may want to start working with Alawashka alone, in a quiet time and location. Alawashka reverberates in the highest frequencies. This means that while you are speaking or singing Alawashka, you are also sending this Divine blessing into your world and aligning your world to the All. Your energetic pattern shifts into one of direct Divine connection. This also occurs within your whole planet. The more you sing or experience Alawashka, the more your personal energies are accelerated. This correlates to shift the energies of all beings on the planet and to the planet Herself.

If you have elected not to begin with ritual, which is fine, and have chosen one of the songs, it is still beneficial to start working alone, and with only one simple song. As you set your space within and without, you will be activating these energies in a natural progression of frequency. I have organized the poems in a sequence that flows well. The first poem's energies build and align with the next, and so on. The sequence creates an energetic pattern that is quite elegant. Each poem has its particular frequency within the greater frequency of the language. They are organized in this manner for your ease. With all this said, choose the songs that move you.

Before you proceed, I recommend that you read through the Alawashka song to understand what energies you will be working with and to familiarize yourself with the language and its translations. Take your time to feel into the song, the words and the frequencies. I suggest you do this with any and every poem in this book, especially when you are selecting a song for work. It will aid you in feeling which energies are dancing towards you, and which you have chosen to embrace. Once you have decided upon your selection and your approach, you are ready to begin. You may add candles, sacred objects and incense if you like. Your joy, quiet and comfort is all that is truly necessary, so include as few or as many special objects and energies as are comfortable to you.

Every aspect of Alawashka is presented as a gift to you. There is no set way to express your connection to the Divine. Follow your own knowing and celebrate your own blessing.

Designing a special ritual around one of these songs would be very powerful indeed. When you are comfortable with the initial poems that open you to the language, you may call upon these in your work. Do this all in grace. Be gentle with yourselves and see the changes unfold.

Please know these songs are for everyone. Even children can enjoy them. When you are including children, and I encourage you to do so, please select the gentlest of energies for them. Later, they will surprise you with which songs they wish to sing.

Pronunciation Key

To facilitate your pronunciation of the words in Alawashka, please consult the following.

AY	day, play
Ä	calm, father
EE	easy, freedom
Ï	innocent, intent
O	open, rose
OO	pool, jewel

SONGS OF JOYOUS AWAKENING

CHANT OF BLESSING

MAYA SIMA LAKA HO
(MÄ-YÄ SEE-MÄ LÄ-KÄ HO)
The living breath is present
in the joyous blessing of the soul.

MAYA SIMA LAKA SO
(MÄ-YÄ SEE-MÄ LÄ-KÄ SO)
The living breath is the blessing
of the soul in joyous oneness.

This song is created for chanting and repetition. It can be spoken or sung at any quiet time. You can read it as a morning prayer to awaken your energies as you go forth in your day and to attune yourself to the presence of the Divine working within you. You can use it as a mantra to create your own meditation, by repeating the phrases over and over until you feel a shift within or a resonant frequency that you wish to feel and explore. It is not a mantra, per se, but can be used in a similar fashion.

You can recite this song before your own meditation practice to heighten your work or to receive the added frequencies of Alawashka within your normal practice. You can also pick this up at any time, day or night and read it silently to receive the blessings, calm and presence of Divine light within.

MAYA SIMA LAKA HO
The living breath is present
in the joyous blessing of the soul.

MAYA is the breath, the Divine inhale and exhale of the All.
SIMA is the greatest joy, a deep rich joy, that can be experienced as bliss.
LAKA is the blessing of the soul, and in this blessing is healing and renewal.
HO is the presence, the now-ness, the here-ness of experience.

This poem has many combinations and underlayments of meaning. The words continue to vary in their definitions. Each word, combined with the others, forms a sentence in which the relationships and meanings quietly move around each other finding alternate alliances. Each word is affiliated with another. They merge. They blend. They compound. They create anew. The frequencies of each word separately and together create a new and meaningful expression.

This dance of energetic association can subtly alter with emphasis and repetition. This process is a frequency of expansion. It has similarities to ancient circle dances, where the movements of the circle are within one direction, but soon, partners are changing, the patterns are moving, expanding and contracting in ever different ways, yet all is still contained within the dance.

MAYA SIMA LAKA HO.

The living breath is present in the joyous blessing of the soul.

MAYA SIMA LAKA HO

The joyous living breath is ever-present in the blessings of the soul.

MAYA SIMA LAKA HO
> The blessing of the soul is the living breath, joyfully present.

MAYA SIMA LAKA HO
> The renewal of the spirit is the joy, fully present in the breath of life.

MAYA SIMA LAKA HO
> The living breath is the blessing of the soul in joyous now-ness.

MAYA, this living breath; *LAKA* is the blessing of the soul; *SIMA*, in joyous; *SO*, oneness.

MAYA SIMA LAKA SO
> Oneness is the joyous blessing of the soul within the living breath.

MAYA SIMA LAKA SO
> Spirit is renewed in the joyous Oneness of the breath of life.

MAYA SIMA LAKA SO
> Joy is the living breath blessing the soul with Oneness.

MAYA SIMA LAKA SO
> The joyful blessing of the soul is the Oneness of the breath of life.

MAYA SIMA LAKA SO
> The living breath is the joyous renewal of the soul in Oneness.

Alawashka is a language of frequencies in dynamic change and acceleration. In certain circumstances, the combination of the words is often more important than their sequence. Each change in meaning or definition gives an added permutation to the acceleration of the vibrations and creates greater openings of experience. Each repetition brings greater energy to the frequencies and alters the expression and the infusion of the words. This reveals the hidden nuances in the language.

Speaking a song as a poem can create energetic shifts as it rises within you. Your inner being will be feeling the vibrational shifting of the subtle movement of the words into a kaleidoscopic energy pattern of expression. This can lead to shifting or opening of subtle realms within you.

You may experience an escalating feeling as you travel within this song. This occurs when you are slowly raising your energies in a certain ratio of progression. You may sense an immediate pulse somewhere within the repetitions. This occurs when you encounter a limitation pattern or a block which is ready to release. You may feel a popping or a whoosh of energy. If you notice this, you have sufficiently raised your personal harmony to open to another level of frequency. Even if you experience none of these sensations, your energy will be accelerating to your highest level.

SHENA ANSHAKA
Calling Forth My Destiny

HO LAKA SHENA WHAL ANSHAKA
(HO LÄ-KÄ SHEE-NÄ WÄL ÄÑ-SHÄ'-KÄ)
I am restored and healed the moment
I recognize the calling forth of my destiny.

HEY ANYA SHOLLA MANYA SICKA
(HAY ÄN-YÄ SHO-LÄ MÄN-YÄ SEEKÄ)
It is the dearest reconnection
of my precious inner peace.

ALA WAKA SHOLTI BALIYA SOLTO
(ÄLÄ WÄ-KÄ SHOL-TEE BÄH-LEE-YÄ SOL-TO)
The sacred dance is evoked
within my rejoicing spirit.

SHA'MAKA SO LA. HA MA. HA MA
(SHAY'-MÄ-KÄ SO LÄ. HAY MAY. HAY MAY)
I am held and enfolded within this oneness of being.
The Goddess is here, the great Mother is here.

SHENA ANSHAKA is a song/poem that creates a resonant link with your personal destiny. As often happens in Earth life, you can sense there is something vital you are to participate within and yet, the force or texture of it eludes you. This poem incorporates your personal vibrational makeup and impetus toward fulfillment and reaches toward the resonant field which holds the greater inspiration of your being. In this way it connects you to your expanded destiny. This destiny becomes a clearer presence in your life.

SHENA ANSHAKA is a repetitive poem, to be recited or sung over and over again to help you ascend to the level wherein you understand your full destiny of being in the universe.

Each of you, as individuals and as a collective, has the unique ability to unite with your full destiny, to reach and transcend the limitations that are seemingly among you. The sacred dance of life is evoked within your rejoicing spirits. When your hearts are full of the beauty and the glory of divinity, the sacred dance is called forth in all its splendor. The movements of the clouds, the stars who delight in your natures, the tides of your ancient waters, all join you in this gift of joy. You reach toward your fullest and the firmaments open to you. You are reconnected to your ancient, future selves. The clarity of your vision is eternity.

As you call forth unto your destiny you are restored to your full stance as beings in this eternal world of glory. Your powers to exist and to create and to destroy are evident. The grace of your beings comes to enfold you. You are held and embraced in the oneness of eternity. You see your nature within this and partake of your Divine wisdom. You become what you already are, and yet cannot fully touch. You return again to the destiny. You return again to the reconnection. You return again to the spirit dance. You return again to the Oneness. You return again to the great Mother of All Beings. And as you continue to sing this song, you return again and again to this womb of existence which has no ties to your destiny, save that you are fully free to embrace it.

This song encompasses the freedom to fly and to be as you fully are. The more often it is sung and chanted, the greater the expression of your divinity unfolds within you. It is so.

Bless you for you are more than you know.

SHENA ANSHAKA
Calling Forth My Destiny

Ho La - ka She-na Whal An -sha - ka

Hey An-ya Shol - la Man - ya Sic - ka

Al - a Wa - ka Shol -ti Bal- i - ya Sol - to

Sha -ma- ka Sol La Ha Ma Ha Ma

Sha -ma- ka Sol La Ha Ma Ha Ma

Al - a Wa - ka Shol- ti Bal- i -ya Sol- to

Sha-ma-ka So La Ha___ Ma

Circle Of Being

HO SHINKTA SHOMATA ANSHKA SHOOLA
(HO-SHEEN-KTÄ SHO-MÄ- TÄ ÄN-SHKÄ SHOO-LÄ)
Here, in the joyful calling forth,
you are invoked into being.

MANACO SHAMPTA ALAWAKA SO
(MÄ-NÄ-KO SHÄM-PTÄ ÄL-Ä-WÄ-KÄ SO)
The sacred place of reclaiming
awaits the oneness of our spirits.

MANYA SHOLTA INXA MANYATTA
(MÄ-NYÄ SHOL-TÄ ÏNK-SÄ MÄN-YÄ-TÄ)
Precious Ones, we call you into the rejoicing
of the endless circle of being.

HONSHA NOWAKU MAYA SHAY'EYA
SHENTA HE LA SO
(HON-SHÄ NO-WÄ-KOO MÄ-YÄ SHAY-EE-YÄ
SHEEN-TÄ HAY LÄ SO)
We call forth unto you
to enter the gracious spirit breath
dancing oneness for you in this moment.

C IRCLE OF BEING is a song of invocation. In this poem you are calling forth and being called forth into the great reclaiming frequencies of the Divine. You are calling to the great beings who hold the circles of awakening, the circles of the sacred. You are calling them into your lives. Your call reverberates through the dimensional realities to find those great ones and create an energetic link. This link is your place in the Divine realms. You are activating this space, knowing that it has been calling to you.

You are also invoked into your greater being through this song. As you call forth to them, they call forth to you. They reclaim you into the circle. They reinforce your being with the blessings of oneness. This oneness is more than a philosophic musing. It is the truth of your being awakening to its presence in the great circles of the Divine.

As you invoke them into your life,
they invoke you into theirs.
The circle of rejoicing oneness
embraces you.
It is so.

Blessing For The People

HASHINKTA ANSHANTI KUMARI
(HÄ-SHEEN-KTÄ ÄN-SHÄN-TEE KOO-MÄ-REE)
May your joyful hearts be renewed and replenished.

MALIKA SHOMATA LAKA HO
(MÄ-LEE-KÄ SHO-MÄ-TÄ LÄ-KÄ HO)
May the miracles of the soul express the wonders
from the highest places, here on this world.

AMTU ANSHA IMPA SALTA
(ÄM-TOO ÄN-SHÄ ÏM-PÄ SÄL-TÄ)
May your calling forth
be sweetly answered in the moment.

HELA MA ALA EMBADO HEYA
(HAY-LÄ MAY ÄLÄ ËM-BÄ-DO HAY-Ä)
May the Goddess be present with you here,
in the heights of your being.

B LESSING FOR THE PEOPLE is a group invocation. This poem is a dedication which can be spoken whenever groups of people gather together. This has been an offering to gathering in various times in Earth chronology. When groups of people gathered to celebrate an event, create ceremony together or hear a speech or important information, this poem was recited as a blessing and invocation for all who gathered.

Alawashka creates. Therefore this "Blessing For The People" creates the fields and frequencies of their greater selves. This invocation declares, creates and holds a vibrational field into which the highest aspects of each individual will be able to be felt, expressed and honored.

HASHINKTA ANSHANTI KUMARI.
May your joyful hearts
be renewed and replenished

Here you call forth the inner joy in each one's heart. You bring the vibrational resonance of joy to each individual. This includes the renewal of Divine blessing and the sweetness of replenishment. This phrase helps each individual feel the energies of the Divine nurturing and filling their hearts.

There are times in life when the sadness of loss is present. When you have the understanding and compassion that all individuals are in a different experience within, then you can call forth the blessings that will restore them.

MALIKA SHOMATA LAKA HO.
May the miracles of the soul express the wonders
from the highest places here on this world.

Once the heart is replenished, the miracles can unfold. This phrase connects the souls of all to the wonders and miracles of life and being. It connects them to the frequencies of the highest vibrational levels and reveals the presence of those miracles, both within each being and also here in this dimensional experience.

AMTU ANSHA IMPA SALTA
May your calling forth
be sweetly answered in the moment

In the presence of renewal, with the expression of the miraculous, the requests may be sweetly answered. In this manner, there is no loss, there is no urgency in any request. There is simply that which is called forth and its sweet reply.

HELA MA ALA EMBADO HEYA.
May the Goddess be present with you here
in the heights of your being.

Now the Goddess may enter. Now the heights of your being may express themselves, for all is taken care of, all is provided. Now the space of blessing can envelop the group and what is to be will gracefully occur.

E ach poem/song is presented to you with these explanations so you can perceive the amplifications and changes in frequencies. Each phrase builds upon the next to gracefully bring the individual to the next level of experience. Each singular word, its placement in the sentence and its position in the whole, creates a relationship of frequencies which provide the individual with the greatest source of Divine expression within the vibrational theme.

Naturally the properties and qualities of each poem/song are different. The theme of each poem is distinctly different. This avails you of the ability to choose the textures of your vibrational experience.

As you work with these poems, you will find an endless variety of vibrational expression within just one song. The theme of each is the invitation which then creates resonances and expansion. Each song will accelerate your being with honor and grace. You need not feel that you have exhausted the frequencies of your chosen song. You could very easily work with one song for the rest of your life and find all the frequencies and accelerations present and available to you. Every song is a revelation of the Divine.

CREATING YOUR PRACTICE

Celebrating a practice is a joyful act of communion. In an Alawashka practice, the intent is to connect with the frequencies of Alawashka and bask in those blessings. This practice is one of many created to invite these energies to participate in your life. The steps to this practice are very simple.

First, find a comfortable quiet place in your home.

Then, center yourself and quiet your mind; give yourself a chance to relax.

Next, address the energies and invite them into the circle of your life to help you to participate in your work.

After this, begin to work in Alawashka by reciting the song or songs in Alawashka you selected. Work with the songs and allow the energies to move within you as you read.

Finally, when you feel ready, open your circle by thanking those who have helped you and release the energies.

Your setting is the sacred space into which the energies will accumulate for your personal work. You create a safe and nurturing space for yourself by centering yourself and connecting with the most blessed energies available. The breathing technique below, will help you center. The setting for your ritual can be anywhere; the time, anytime. Just find a comfortable place in your home. When you are preparing for a ritual it is imperative that you are undisturbed and have very quiet surroundings. This is your time.

To convene your practice and set your space with energies of grace, begin by addressing the four directions and inviting their energies to help you. I address the four directions in this ritual to honor this beautiful planet and the life you live here. Each direction will be addressed and honored as will the great Goddess. You may call in or invite the great beings that you work with to enter the circle and join in the ceremony. These could be your guides, angels, ancestors or names of ancient ones with whom you feel a connection. Adapt this practice to a format that is in keeping with your personal comfort and beliefs. If any of this is uncomfortable, choose not to include it.

Once the circle has been created, it is optimal that you remain within it until your practice is complete. Imagine that you have created a temple of light within your home, and all the Blessed Ones you have invited are there. Bring whatever you think you will need, and get ready to begin. You may stand or sit when you address the directions. It is advisable to speak all of the blessings and all of the poems aloud. Your voice is an honoring and a delight to the Blessed Ones.

Once you have completed your interdimensional invitations, start working with the Alawashka song you have chosen. In this practice, I have selected one song. You may select another song from those listed, if you wish, or you may include more than one song.

Repeat this song as often and as long as you feel appropriate. You may sense the energies build and then wane. You may just know when you're done. Whenever you feel complete, you are complete. This means you are finished with the practice. All that is left is for you to say farewell to those you have invited into the realms of light. Then, of course, enjoy the energies that you feel.

CENTERING YOURSELF

Take a slow, deep breath and relax.

Feel the center of your being as a calm and nurturing spot within your body. Imagine yourself as though the gentle waters of a clear stream are bathing your whole being.

Take another very slow, deep breath.

Sense your connection with all of life. Feel the flow of life and grace flowing inside.

Feel the quiet joy of life moving within you, flowing gently through your whole being.

Take another very slow, very deep breath.

Feel the knowing within you. Feel the inner wisdom that is always present. This knowing is a sacred part of your life. This knowing is the beauty that you carry within. Gently focus on this feeling and know that you are a deep and sacred part of the Universal All.

CREATING THE CIRCLE

Stand or sit facing East, and turn to each direction as it is called.

"Sacred energies of the East, I honor you. I call you to my circle to celebrate Alawashka with me. Bring forth the blessings of the morning light, and the great intelligence of the All. Bring forth the Inspiration of the Winds and the Breath of the Goddess. It is so.

"Sacred energies of the South, I honor you. I call you to my circle to celebrate Alawashka with me. Bring forth the blessings of the full daylight, and the strength and passion of the All. Bring forth the Illuminating Fires and the Eternal Flame of the Goddess. It is so.

"Sacred energies of the West, I honor you. I call you to my circle to celebrate Alawashka with me. Bring forth the Blessings of the Sunset and the Unconditional Love of the All. Bring forth the Flow of the Waters and the Liquid Light of the Goddess.

"Sacred energies of the North, I honor you. I call you to my circle to celebrate Alawashka with me. Bring forth the blessings of the Darkest Midnight and the Abundance of the All. Bring forth the Richness of the Earth and Deep Wisdom of the Goddess. It is so.

"Blessed Goddess, I honor you. I call you into my circle to celebrate Alawashka with me. Bring forth the blessings and energies of Divine connection and frequency, that I may know You and my full self in greater Light. Bring me the greater understanding, that I may celebrate the joy of the All. She is here. It is so."

This next personal addition is optional.

*"Blessed Ones, (insert the names of those divine beings you wish to include or ask for help and guidance), I honor you. I call you into my circle to celebrate the blessings of life and of spirit. I ask for your help and guidance." (You may also ask for help in specific areas of your life at this time, but be clear, specific and brief in what you ask.)

Take a deep breath and feel the richness of the space you have created. Sense how each energy has come into your circle and is offering you the blessings that you have asked. When you feel the shift of energies and the sense of the blessings, begin to sing or recite the song(s) you have chosen. Repeat the song a minimum of three times, or until you feel the energies build and reach their full peak.

THE GALATA
The Milk Of The Universe

ACALA ISHA MAYA HO
(Ä-KÄ-LÄ EE-SHÄ MÄ-YÄ HO)
The breath of life flows to all.

ANAKA WHAL HALUKA
(Ä-NÄ-KÄ WHÄL HÄ-LOO'-KÄ)
The first sensation is wonder, then pleasure.

ALA SICKA MAYA HO
(ÄLÄ SEE-KÄ MÄ-YÄ HO)
The breath within is the peace in-keeping.

ANAKA WHAL HALUKA
(Ä-NÄ-KÄ WHÄL HÄ-LOO'-KÄ)
The first sensation is wonder, then pleasure.

The origin is the joy
which created intent and brings in flow.

What is the river,
but the running of water,
laughing to reach itself again.

The pure existence of being
is one of peace and the flow of creation.
This is the universe existent within me
as I live my life.
For I am the breath of Goddess/God
created into consciousness.

211

I create in a moment.
The universal principal of creation
is present within me for my use.

This is how we are have come into being.
We have been gifted and therefore take our personal essence
from the collective pool of life;
the pool of the souls of all.

I return to the Oneness that is my source.
It is perfection in design.

This inward breath mentioned is actually the breath of the cosmic life force. We call it the liquid light. This is the full range of life force for the All. It manifests in the energetic patterns of the universe. It gives us the higher vibration of our existence. It is the ingestion of life force that creates all life in all vibrational realms.

The out-breath is the release of that energy of life that creates the other miracle. That is of returning to the All. It can be considered the span of one's existence in the godhood. The in-breath is the span of life that is individual and collective. The out-breath is the voyage home to the All. This is the dance of the universe as created by Goddess. The first sensation is wonder. That is the miracle of existence experienced by God and other dimensional beings at the experience of knowing in the light. Then pleasure... This is the supreme joy of being part of the creation, being enabled to be of Goddess, to see through Her eyes and then through our own.

THE GALATA
The Milk Of The Universe

As with all songs, please feel free to harmonize and add your inner expression. This song is created to be sung numerous times to reach an energy peak of celebration and awakening.

COMPLETION OF THE PRACTICE

The Alawashka practice is completed when you finish reciting this song and acknowledge the Universal All for this blessing. It is time for the energies and Blessed Ones that you have called forth to be acknowledged and appreciated for their gifts. They have given you their special gifts and you have shared your ceremony with them. The honoring is mutual. And as they are your esteemed guests, you make it easy and graceful for them to depart.

"Sacred energies of the East, I honor you. I thank you for joining my circle and celebrating Alawashka with me. I have received the blessings of the morning light, and inhaled the great intelligence of the All. I have accepted the inspiration of the winds and flew with the breath of the Goddess. I appreciate all of the gifts you have bestowed. I hold you in the dearest blessings of my heart and release your energies from this circle. It is so.

"Sacred energies of the South, I honor you. I thank you for joining my circle and celebrating Alawashka with me. I have received the blessings of the full daylight, and the strength and passion of the All. I have accepted the illuminating fires and danced with the eternal flame of the Goddess. I hold you in the dearest blessings of my heart and release your energies from this circle. It is so.

"Sacred energies of the West, I honor you. I thank you for joining my circle and celebrating Alawashka with me. I have received the blessings of the sunset and drank the unconditional love of the All. I have accepted the flow of the waters and swam in the liquid light of the Goddess. I hold you in the dearest blessings of my heart and release your energies from this circle. It is so.

"Sacred energies of the North, I honor you. I thank you for joining my circle and celebrating Alawashka with me. I have received the blessings of the darkest midnight and tasted the abundance of the All. I have accepted the richness of the Earth and deep wisdom of the Goddess. I hold you in the dearest blessings of my heart and release your energies from this circle. It is so.

Blessed Goddess, I honor you. I thank you for joining my circle and celebrating Alawashka with me. I have received the blessings and energies of Divine connection and frequency. I have felt you and known you and my inner self in the greater Light. I have accepted the greater understanding you have shared, and celebrate the joy of the All. I hold you in the dearest blessings of my heart and release your energies from this circle. It is so.

This next personal addition is optional.

* Blessed Ones, I honor you. I thank you for joining my circle. I thank you for the gifts of help and guidance that you have bestowed. I hold you in the dearest blessings of my heart and release your energies from this circle. It is so.

Your practice is complete.

Fly open-armed into your life.
Receive the sanctuary of your soul.
Expand in the graceful flow of energies that fill you.
Embrace the gifts of the Divine.

Blessings on your journey
and
blessings on your homing.

Shona Halwaku
Emerge Dancing

My greatest blessing to you
on your journey
into the Heart of the Universe.
May your being soar
with the beauty, grace, joy and full expression
of the Goddess and the Divine,
in every moment.
Blessed be.

As you learn of your ancient legacy and spiritual destiny, let your heart and awareness fly free. See your journeys through time, space and consciousness as the great blessing of Divine experience. Bring your minds to the lands of wisdom, where truth rings symphonies of revelation. You could not be on this path, if your roads in time and awakening had not led here. Heal and liberate your past by honoring your passage.

As you enact the rituals, say the words, hear the sounds, and open to the touch of Alawashka, the voice of the miraculous will touch your cheek and annoint your heart. This is the time you have waited so very long to hold. You are here, in this moment to fill the universe with your awakening.

As you learn the frequencies of creation and sound the music and poems of Alawashka, let your soul and inner knowing embrace the flows of energy that come to fill your sails. For you are great travelers in the seas of consciousness. Your awakening, your joyous stretch into the connecting fibers of the Great All, fills the halls of light with rapture.

I share this language through blessing. I, too, have waited for aeons that were but a moment, to hear your voices chime with the language of creation. I am here as a sign of awakening to your being, to your heart, to your soul, to your mind. I am here to help you follow the great flows of energy that link all times in a great circle of illumination.

Speak me. Sing me. Laugh me into your hearts where the breath of the universe can unfurl in wonders. Bring the forces of creation into your lives. Weave the threads of remarkable brilliance into a tapestry that you dream to live. Open the doors of time, reclaim your past, uplift your present and bring the full glory of Divine Spirit into your future.

The future is your now. The future is your now.

The future is your now.

Glossary

Alamorro:
Beings created by Anshamaya. Those of Divine intelligence and joy, not in materialized form.

Alawashka:
The original language of creation. The being, language, music and frequency which organizes all form into existence.

Annunaki:
Beings created by the Wannashama. Visited Earth while the Lyrans were here.

Anshamaya:
The first creator gods and goddesses organized into awareness by the intention of the Goddess and the organization of Alawashka.

Anshara:
Esteemed member of the Council. Intervened for humanity in the original genetic experiments.

Gateway:
Galactic Heart Matrix, the Heart of the Goddess. The energetic passageway through which higher frequencies enter our planet.

Goddess:
The Universal Source of All.

Lyrans:
Beings created by the Wannashama. First group of beings to stay upon the planet. Much younger distant cousins of the Shatowa.

Pleiadians:
Beings created by the Wannashama; Visited Earth while the Lyrans were here.

Shatowa:
Beings created by the Wannashama, the first beings to walk upon this planet. The Shatowa are awareized consciousness, not in physical form.

Shollamaya Frequency:
The Goddess' Dynamic Resonant Frequency Accelerated Alignment. Shollamaya means "Reconnecting Breath."

Sirians:
Beings created by the Wannashama. Visited Earth while the Lyrans were here.

Terra Gaia:
The Earth.

The Council:
A collection of very high frequency beings, who attend to the matters of the universe to help the full expression and evolution of all being.

Wannashama:
Timeless beings, created by Alamorro. The Wannashama are the creators of this universal focus.

ABOUT THE AUTHOR

Lumari is an author, psychic, channel and spiritual teacher. For over twenty years she has provided professional psychic and spiritual consulting and life coaching services for both national and international clients.

Lumari is a featured guest on radio and is listed in Who s Who in America and the world. She conducts workshops and celebrations in Alawashka, spiritual discovery, ritual and transformation.

Lumari connects with the highest frequencies of Divine Source and brings those messages to us through her books, tapes, spiritual artwork and private consultations. Her channeled Alawashka Soul Song readings bring illumination and inspiration to her clients. Lumari is available for private consultations, speaking engagements and workshops.

To contact Lumari for a private consultation, to attend the Alawashka Gatherings and workshops or to schedule your Alawashka Soul Song reading please write to her at

Amethyst
c/o 7 Avenida Vista Grande, Suite B7-113
Santa Fe, New Mexico PZ [87508]
blessings@lumari.com
Visit her websites
www.lumari.com   www.amethystplanet.com

Resources

For Lumari s books, sacred art, audio tapes, workshops and upcoming events and for healing and meditation music by Peter Bried, please contact your local bookstore, use our order form, visit our website or please send a stamped, self addressed #10 envelope to: Amethyst
    c/o 7 Avenida Vista Grande, Suite B7-113
    Santa Fe, New Mexico PZ [87508]

Akashic Records:
Collective Keepers of Divine Expression
by Lumari
Learn about the Akashic Records from the beings who hold the wisdom of the ages. The Akashic Records are an ancient collective of beings who hold all of the universal knowledge. Channeled by Lumari, the Keepers of the Akashic share the wisdom held within their care, discuss their system, its workings and ways to access the vast resources of the records of consciousness they have collected and contained for all time.
$12.00

Alawashka Paths to Awakening
by Lumari
Align with Your True Destiny and Expand Your Divine Connection! Experience your continual joy, healing and spiritual communion through the extraordinary resonance of Alawashka songs and practices. Receive blessing, healing and heart-felt Divine energy. Learn to flow in harmony with the energies of creation.
    Listen to the Paths of Awakening CD, today. These two empowering meditations, Calling Destiny and Goddess Breath will put you on the path of your inner purpose and spiritual growth.
$21.95 CD

Alawashka
by Lumari
In *Alawashka*, Lumari connects us with the most awe-inspiring discovery of our times. This compelling exploration of humanity, universal healing and transformation is told by Alawashka, the voice of creation. Both a language and a being, Alawashka initiates our spiritual awakening and activates the highest expression of

love, spirituality and inner peace. Experiencing these energies of creation will change your life.
$21.95

Universal Suite
by Peter Bried
Healing and Meditation Music. Powerful and uplifting music composed and created in communion with the Divine. Touch the highest realms. Travel within the joyful expansion of the Universe and receive the Divine blessings of your journey.
Listen to samples of Peter s music on the web. www.amethyst.cc
$16.00 CD

Alawashka Gatherings with Lumari
Celebrate the Sacred Flows of Creation
Awaken to your personal destiny and universal purpose. Experience profound healing and spiritual growth. Benefit from intensive individual work and a direct, transformative experience of the sacred. Learn to expand the sacred power of your own life and contribute to the healing and evolution of our world. Through Alawashka teachings and practices, meditations and energy work you will move you into a profound connection to the Divine. Come, join us and experience the resonance of the Alawashka.

Amethyst Catalog
View our complete online cataloue of Lumari s books, music, audio and Sacred Geometry art prints, Peter Bried s music and Alawashka items visit www.AmethystPlanet.com

Alawashka Soul Song: Your Sacred Soul Song
by Lumari
Your Soul Song creates an opening, an ongoing connection with your full being and the Divine. It is the song your soul longs to sing to express your highest resonace, joy and purpose. Your Soul Song connects you with your true destiny.

Receive your personal Alawashka Soul Song, in poem form, channeled in Alawashka and its English translation beautifully printed and suitable for framing. Also included is a special channeling from Alawashka about your song.

To schedule, please contact Lumari at the above address
email blessings@lumari.com
visit www.lumari.com

AMETHYST ORDER FORM

Please Print

First Name _____

Last Name _____

Street _____

City _____ State _____

Country _____ Postal Code _____

Phone _____

Email _____

Check/Money Order ☐   Credit Card   MC ☐   VISA ☐   AMEX ☐   JBC ☐

CC Number [_____]   Exp. [_____]

Signature [_____]

Please include me on your mailing list. ☐

Where did you purchase this book? _____

Quantity	Title	Price	Total
	Akashic Records	$12.00	
	Alawashka: Paths to Awakening CD	$21.95	
	Alawashka	$21.95	
	Universal Suite by Peter Bried CD	$16.00	
	Amethyst Catalogue (include SASE)	*Free!*	
	Subtotal plus Shipping (see below)		
	TOTAL DUE		

Payment: Checks & Credit cards **payable to BLUE STAR Network**.
Payment must be by credit card or USA currency only.
Shipping and Handling: Allow 1-3 weeks for delivery, no CODs.
Books & music: USA and Canada include $4.00 for first item and $1.50 for each
additional item. International orders please include $11.00 for Global Priority
Shipping or write for shipping costs.

Amethyst
c/o 7 Avenida Vista Grande, Suite B7-113
Santa Fe, New Mexico PZ [87508]
www.amethystplanet.com
Visit Lumari online at www.lumari.com

Order Books & CD s here - or - Online at www.AmethystPlanet.com